I've Got Your Back

Help Children Say

Hello to Friends & Goodbye to Bullies

LORNA BLUMEN, MS, MBA & STACI SCHWARTZ, MD

Camberley Press

Library of Congress Cataloging-in-Publication Data (US)

Names: Blumen, Lorna, author. | Schwartz, Staci, author.

Title: I've Got Your Back: Help Children Say Hello to Friends & Goodbye to Bullies / Lorna Blumen and Staci Schwartz

Description: Toronto, ON: Camberley Press Ltd, 2016. | Summary: Empower kids of all ages to stop bullying and let them know that caring adults will always have their backs. Age-appropriate children's stories and skill-building activities, along with adult-focused material, help parents and teachers guide children to build positive, respectful friendships, stick up for one another, and develop empathy and self-esteem. Developed for children ages 5-10. These skills and concepts apply for all ages requiring support and skill-building in bullying prevention and improving friendships.

ISBN 978-0-9810589-5-5 (paperback)

Subjects: LCSH: Bullying. | Bullying in schools. | Parenting. | School environment. | Interpersonal relations. BISAC: FAMILY & RELATIONSHIPS / Bullying. | FAMILY & RELATIONSHIPS / Conflict Resolution. | FAMILY & RELATIONSHIPS / Friendship. | FAMILY & RELATIONSHIPS / Parenting / General.

Classification: LCC: BF637.B85B576 2016 | DDC 302.343——dc23

Library and Archives Canada Cataloguing in Publication

Blumen, Lorna, author. Schwartz, Staci, author.

I've Got Your Back: Help Children Say Hello to Friends & Goodbye to Bullies/ Lorna Blumen & Staci Schwartz

ISBN 978-0-9810589-5-5 (paperback)

1. Bullying in schools--Prevention. I. Schwartz, Staci II. Title.

LB3013.3.B58 2016   371.5'8   C2016-902936-0

For bulk purchase discounts, please contact CamberleyPress.com.

All facts, figures, and websites were verified as of October 2015. If you find an error, please contact CamberleyPress.com.

Cover Design: Lisa Hochstein, Christine Magday

Interior Design and Layout: Christine Magday

Illustrations: Staci Schwartz

Photos: istockphoto.com

10 9 8 7 6 5 4 3 2 1

Printed in the United States of America

Camberley Press Ltd
PO Box 74553
Toronto, ON, Canada M9A 3T0
CamberleyPress.com

Contents

1

Welcome to Parents

For Adults

It's Back-to-School Time Again!

As we say goodbye to summer, most kids look forward to back-to-school shopping, seeing their friends, meeting new teachers, and being one of the "big kids" at school. It can be a time of great excitement. For some kids, however, going back to school brings feelings of dread: *Will I have friends? Will I be picked on (again) this year? Will I be excluded from the popular group? Will I be safe at recess?* Did you notice that, *Will I be great at math?* isn't on the list?

As you prepare your child for the new school year, remember that the most important supplies you can put in his or her backpack are your love and support. Let your child know you'll be there when he or she needs you— with schoolwork, making and keeping friends, trying new activities and sports—whatever the new year brings. **Let your child know you'll always have their back.**

You Asked, We Answered

This book is designed to answer the question parents and teachers ask us most often: *What can I do to protect my child (or a child in my class) from bullying?* As bullying prevention specialists with more than 30 years of experience, we want adults who love and work with kids to know that there are many easy things parents and teachers can do to build kids' social skills, self-esteem, and empathy. This solid foundation helps make kids bully-resistant.

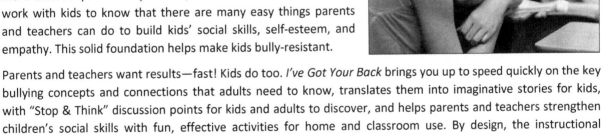

Parents and teachers want results—fast! Kids do too. *I've Got Your Back* brings you up to speed quickly on the key bullying concepts and connections that adults need to know, translates them into imaginative stories for kids, with "Stop & Think" discussion points for kids and adults to discover, and helps parents and teachers strengthen children's social skills with fun, effective activities for home and classroom use. By design, the instructional components are short and easy-to-use so busy parents, teachers, and kids feel supported, not overwhelmed.

This quick-start action guide can be used by all adults who work with kids, including parents, teachers, teaching assistants, guidance counselors, coaches, mental health professionals, family physicians, and pediatricians. The beginning of school is the ideal time to establish bullying prevention guidelines, but it's never too late to press the reset button.

Why is Bullying Prevention So Important?

How we treat other people and how we are treated by other people has a profound influence on our hearts and minds. These social interactions determine our view of the world. When we (as children or adults) feel happy, safe, and trust that we will be treated with respect, kindness, and fairness (for the most part), our self-esteem is boosted and we are more likely to treat others that way, too. When something unfair happens, we are resilient enough to heal the hurt and move on.

The reverse is true, too. If our self-esteem is shaky and we expect to be treated badly, our vision narrows to focus on those negative experiences, giving them more weight than they deserve and coloring our future expectations. We feel defensive and we might treat others badly right from the start, in a misguided attempt to protect ourselves from further hurt. When we teach kids the skills to resolve conflicts and treat one another with respect and empathy, they will be better able to handle life's ups and downs.

Bullying prevention is about much more than children's school-based bullying. It's about inclusivity at every level of society—how to welcome newcomers into our increasingly complex, multicultural neighborhoods, how to relate positively with others at school and at work, despite differences in experience and opinion, and how to persist and solve international conflicts before they explode into human tragedy and crisis. It's an interconnected web. You may think you're only focusing on the piece marked "kids' bullying prevention," but you quickly see it's only a few links away from every other social issue. It's so much easier to build healthy coping skills when kids are young to prevent or soften these impossible-to-solve adult problems.

How to Use This Book

I've Got Your Back is primarily geared for parents and children ages 5–10. Teachers and other professionals will also find this book useful. Chapters 1, 2, and 3, written for adults, are for parents and teachers to read on their own. These chapters discuss the key issues and challenges with children's friendships and bullying. Chapter 4, written for children, contains stories of friendship and bullying. Adults and children should read this chapter together. Chapter 5 contains activities for parents and children, or teachers and students, to enjoy together. Chapter 6, written for adults, outlines future steps for building an enduring culture of kindness. Finally, Chapter 7 contains resources for further learning.

The one-on-one parent-child activities can be scaled to include an entire class, depending on the needs and strengths of the students and the specific bullying prevention issues you're working to prevent or resolve. Older and younger children can also benefit from these ideas and activities.

Bullying: It's a Fact of Life (For Now)

Bullying affects adults and children of all ages, genders, races, religious and cultural backgrounds, appearances, abilities, and income levels. Bullying of and by children is an infectious, damaging, and sometimes deadly problem that must be controlled. There's an epidemic of unkind treatment in schools set within a social culture of cruelty. Humiliation is now a form of entertainment, on TV and in person. Peers often don't help, and adults rarely get involved until there's a serious problem and damage has already been done.

The statistics on kids' bullying are disheartening. In a recent national survey, 16% of kids in grades 3–12 reported being bullied, while another 14% fear being bullied. Approximately 16% of girls and 17% of boys revealed that they were verbally bullied at least 2–3 times a month. Fifty-one percent of targeted students said they had been bullied for six months or more, and 39% said that the bullying lasted for a year or longer.[1] Bullying may still be underreported—the definitions continue to change and kids are often discouraged from reporting bullying.

Cyberbullying: A 24/7 Problem

That's not all. In the days before technology put smartphones in our hands, targets of school yard bullying found peace and safety at home. Today, bullying starts at school and continues after school and online. Targeted kids can receive thousands of hurtful messages via social media. Bullying is now 24/7, with a dangerous downside.

Cyberbullying is a hot topic, for good reason. A recent review found 23% of children ages 12–18 reported being cyberbullied.[2] Kids' cyberbullying typically remains hidden much longer than other types of bullying, coming into adult awareness as a full-blown emergency with full media attention. While we certainly need to jump into protective action at the first sign of crisis, adults must understand bullying's building blocks to prevent future life-threatening crises.

Cyberbullying is often treated as a stand-alone entity, ignoring its crucial connection to face-to-face bullying. If adults have not set—and enforced—consistent behavioral limits for how kids treat one another in person, behavior will only get worse online due to the lack of adult supervision and kids' false sense of online anonymity.[3]

Vulnerable teens have committed suicide when unable to cope with the overwhelming exposure to negative comments, taunts, and threats. And while that may seem unimaginably far from where your young children are today, that path is paved day-by-day and step-by-step by allowing meanness and humiliation to be acceptable in our interactions with other human beings.

Bullying Hurts Everyone, Not Just the Target

Everyone is damaged by bullying—bullies, targets, and bystanders (both adults and kids). School-wide academic performance suffers and we now know that the damage to kids can last far beyond a single incident or school year. The damage to hearts and brains can last for a lifetime.

Being a bullied target or a frequent bystander to bullying is a lonely and frightening experience for kids. Bullying is also upsetting to parents. For too many children and parents, fear is a daily ingredient of school life. For these kids, it's less about preparing for a math test and more about surviving the day without experiencing name-calling, shaming, physical interference, or exclusion from peer groups of *frenemies*.

Once a bullying problem surfaces, parents and adults at school are inconsistently successful at stopping it, often unsure when to intervene. Some schools are more responsive than others, but it takes a committed effort by every staff person to be on the lookout for bullying. Bullying prevention needs an "all hands on deck" approach. Each day's incidents must be addressed with both short- and long-term follow-up.

Prevention is the key. While adults must help kids deal with bullying when it happens, the only real solution is to stop bullying before it starts. We can encourage kids to form positive friendships, develop relationships with children outside of school (camps, clubs, hobby groups, church/synagogue/mosque youth groups), and feel empowered and less isolated by focusing on their talents and strengths.

Parents must be involved from the beginning and work at home to change behavior and connect with our kids. Schools need to pay attention consistently once a bullying problem surfaces. Addressing it once won't resolve the issue. Even a bullying episode which has been "handled" still requires ongoing low-level monitoring, at school and at home, to be alert to recurrences. Kids will get the message that adults are serious about bullying prevention.

Children's bullying prevention is everybody's responsibility. Kids must have resilience, and there will be ups and downs in life, but we can no longer afford to think that bullying is a normal part of growing up.

The Good News

It's not all bad news. We can turn this around.

Adults must do a better job standing up to protect kids, unwaveringly insisting on kindhearted, respectful behavior between kids and their peers and between adults and kids—in all directions.

Far better outcomes occur, with much less damage, if we intervene at the first signs of bullying and work harder on prevention than on punishment. Bullying's daily building-block behaviors are often accepted or ignored. The downside of looking the other way is costly.

Teaching kids the skills of friendship, even and *especially* during conflict, is necessary to change the lives and outcomes for bullies, targets, and bystanders. When adults take the lead, kids will step up and become outspoken *upstanders*—learning to protect their friends and stand up for the rights of those with less power, skill, or ability. From this perspective, they will be more likely to welcome newcomers, take responsibility for mistakes, and work to change their schools, communities, and the world.

Children and their parents need to feel secure in the knowledge that kids will be cherished and cared for in schools that safeguard every child's right to learn in a school environment of emotional and physical safety. **We want children to know that parents and teachers have their backs.**

The Importance of Positive Friendships

Positive friendships protect and insulate kids from many issues, including bullying. Kids need kind, respectful, empathic friends who know how to have fun, tease (not taunt or bully), share confidences, support dreams, and provide comfort and encouragement. Having friends creates a sense of belonging. Having peers to talk to helps kids rebound more quickly from stress and bumps in the road.

Our children's friends have a huge impact on their behavior, self-esteem, values, goals, and big life choices right from the early years. If children learn how to identify positive relationships and build self-esteem when they're young, the chances of kids gravitating toward destructive relationships later in life will be minimized.[4][5]

Bullying Prevention Can Be Simple

In an ideal world, as soon as a bullying problem arose, adults would jump to attention and say: *OMG, we had no idea! Thanks for letting us know. We're so glad we caught this early. The adults at home and school will work together on this. We're going to remind the children of our values, our expectations for their behavior, and model positive behavior for them. We will do a more consistent job of monitoring the kids and intervening at the first sign of additional mistakes.* The adults would then keep their word, correct the immediate situation, and monitor the children's interactions at a low level for the next several months to make sure the problem doesn't recur.

How often do you recall a bullying problem being solved that early? Or simply?

In the early stages, bullying prevention is straightforward. At the first sign of unkindness or bullying behavior, an adult should encourage the misbehaving child to choose different words or behavior: *We treat everyone with respect. Can you please say that in a nicer way?* Speak to the child with a smile or a neutral face, not with a scowl or in anger. The goal is to give the child a chance to improve under the watchful and helpful eyes of an adult.

The bottom line in bullying prevention is actually pretty simple: You don't have to love everybody and you don't have to be everyone's best friend, but you MUST make a place for everyone and treat everyone with respect, even and *especially* during conflict.

Bullying: Whose Problem Is It?

The responsibility for decreasing children's bullying should be shared by all. Adults, however, have the primary responsibility for prevention, control, and monitoring, making sure that kids operate within the boundaries consistently. Children absolutely have roles and responsibilities in bullying prevention, but children cannot do their jobs if adults don't do ours.

Please remember: The ONLY solution to bullying is prevention. Realistically, it's not possible to eliminate bullying completely. Instead, we must focus on early intervention, setting boundaries, and minimizing the negative effects. Preventive, low-level behavior monitoring is a permanent responsibility for all adults who work or live with kids. Yes, mistakes will be made and they must be handled. Genuine apologies and repairs must be offered when someone gets hurt—even when the hurt was unintentional. Every mistake is a strong reminder to increase our prevention efforts. Failing to respond sows the seeds of the next crisis.

Adults Also Suffer When Kids Are Bullied

Parents worry when they see their children excluded from playdates and birthday parties, cut off from friendships, and fearful of going to school. As the problem worsens, parents become concerned for their children's safety and mental health.

Teachers' stress rises when working in bullying environments. Entire classrooms can be disrupted. Teachers are distracted by numerous discipline problems and must focus on mediating relationships between students instead of teaching. Students fall behind academically.

When a school has a kids' bullying problem, there's a good chance there's also workplace bullying among the staff. Adults dread going to work in environments like this. Reducing bullying benefits everyone.

My Child is Already Being Bullied. Is it Too Late?

It's never too late to stop or repair a bullying situation. It's much easier to prevent or catch it early, but kids need help all the way through. While the start of a new school year is the perfect time to set ground rules to prevent bullying, the ideas in this book also apply to ongoing problems. See Chapter 7's list of books for adults about children's bullying prevention and Chapter 5's recommended books for children about friendship.

What We Bring to the Table

Lorna Blumen, MS, MBA brings 20 years of experience as a children's and adult workplace bullying prevention specialist. She's a speaker, educational consultant, and author of five books on children's bullying prevention and girls' respect issues, including *Bullying Epidemic: Not Just Child's Play* and *Girls' Respect Groups: An Innovative Program To Empower Young Women & Build Self-Esteem!* Lorna was also a contributing author to two books on business leadership and children's mental health. She is the lead developer of the Girls' Respect Groups Program, an after-school program for girls 10–18. The GRG Program is used in the US, Canada, and 130 countries. Her websites, BullyingEpidemic.com and GirlsRespectGroups.com, provide international connections and bullying prevention resources.

Staci Schwartz, MD is a physician, author, and illustrator of children's books who has worked for the past 10 years as an educational consultant on bullying prevention strategies for elementary school-aged children. She has channeled her many talents and experience into the creation of two sparkling, humorous, and gently educational anti-bullying books for children: *Billy the Baaadly Behaving Bully Goat* and *The New Bear on the Block*. Her interactive readings and bullying prevention workshops have trained many children—and their teachers—to be alert to and proactive in addressing the signs of bullying. Her work has helped children develop empathy, increase their self-esteem, and promote respect for their classmates. Staci has also facilitated workshops for educators about teaching tolerance in the classroom using bibliotherapy and engaging games and activities.

What You Bring to the Table

Parents, teachers, and all adults who work with kids genuinely want bullying stopped or reduced significantly. We want children to form strong friendships with kids who accept them for who they are and to treat one another with kindness and respect. This requires adult support. We must instill these values in our kids and lead by example.

Parents and teachers are on the front line, dealing with bullying prevention every day. Adults have the power to restore peace and security—for our kids and ourselves. With some guidance, we can recognize bullying in the early stages, intervene with kindness and firmness to stop it early, and build the skills of resilience to help kids rebound from life's ups and downs. Thank you for joining us in this important work.

A Note About Labels

All kids—and adults—misbehave occasionally. We ask you to see bullying as behavior-based, not as a permanent label for a child. A child exhibiting bullying behavior is not destined to be a lifelong bully, nor is a target of bullying sure to be a lifelong victim.

A child who acts like a bully can begin to change substantially in a month with effort and support. Bystanders, and even kids who have been targets, can become upstanders. Let's approach all children and their problems with hope for change and clear statements about the positive behavior we wish to see in the future. We must make room, in our schedules and our hearts, for a child to grow and change.

As a first step, we can change our language. Instead of saying, *Sean's a bully,* let's say, *Sean acted like a bully when he tripped Mike.* Describe the problematic behavior: *Not letting Elise sit with you and your friends at lunch was unkind. You were acting like a bully.* Give children words they can use: *Donato's acting like a bully; he pushed me.* When we use the words "bully," "target," or "bystander" in this book, we are referring to behavior, not labeling individuals.

We have alternated the use of "him" and "her" throughout this book. It's another reminder that bullying and target behaviors can be found in both boys and girls. We have also included the use of "they" to reflect our changing awareness of the spectrum of gender identity, which can surface very early in young children. We ask you to discuss this issue with your children in an age- and experience-appropriate manner.

Can This (or Any) Book Stop Bullying Altogether?

Not likely. Conflict is a normal part of life, and different opinions make life interesting. Not all conflict involves bullying, but it can be easy to cross the line. Every social situation has the potential for bullying.

Schools are too frequently blamed for kids' bullying. Anywhere kids come together, without consistent and secure boundaries for how to treat others, bullies can rule. Because kids spend most of their time in social groups at school, we see the majority of kids' bullying in this environment. That doesn't mean schools are the cause of kids' bullying. But schools—and the adults inside—play a crucial role in bullying prevention.

Adults must set clear limits, monitor consistently, and teach and model the behavior we want to see. When kids know adults are serious and unwavering about the message "No Bullying Here," they will learn the rules and operate (mostly) within the guidelines.

We hope *I've Got Your Back* will build feelings of trust, safety, and security between parent and child, and between teacher and students. We want parents and teachers to stop blaming one another and to treat one another as allies. The activities in this book are designed to build appreciation and empathy. Using them, we hope you will discover new things about each other—and yourselves.

Even when an adult cannot immediately stop the bullying in a child's life, when a child knows that a caring adult has their back, it insulates and protects the child from the psychologically damaging effects of bullying. This works whether your child or student is behaving as a bully, a target, or a bystander.

Let's Begin

Every home, school, and community has a different starting point, with unique strengths and weaknesses. Use this book as a guide, and adapt the materials and activities to the needs of your child or teaching environment. Send us your best ideas and share your stories and we'll post them to our online communities—a worldwide network of adults and kids working to limit the damaging effects of uncurbed bullying and meanness (info@IGYBBook.com). Working together, each doing our part, huge change can happen. Every day is important.

So with our mothers' hearts and our combined efforts of over 30 years of working to empower and safeguard children, we offer this book to you. Use it to make real change in your world, sending out the message of peace, respect, love, protection, and care to our children and far beyond.

With respect,

Lorna & *Staci*

2

Bullying Essentials for Parents

Getting on the Same Page About Bullying Prevention

Before going further, it's important for us to crystallize the key facts and concepts about bullying. Adults should have a common understanding of what bullying is—and isn't. Surprisingly, we're still struggling with a lack of consistency in the ways we identify and solve bullying problems. Is it bullying or conflict? Teasing or taunting? Tattling or telling? Uncertainty freezes us into inaction, and inaction allows the problem to escalate, giving us a bigger and more difficult problem to untangle. Let's get clear.

What is Bullying?

Bullying is characterized by:

- A persistent, one-way power imbalance where the bully has all the power and the target has none. The roles do not reverse.

- The deliberate use of power and aggression by the bully toward the target.

- The intent to hurt the target physically, socially, or emotionally; often a combination.

- The intent to isolate the target.

- The intent to embarrass and humiliate.

- The intent to cause fear of current and future attacks.

- Repeated attacks, but don't ignore a one-time occurrence.

- Escalating intensity with recurrence.

- Contempt and a lack of empathy for others.

- A sense of entitlement—that's it's acceptable to hurt or treat others in a demeaning manner.

- An underlying lack of respect for self and others.

- Frequent attempts to misdirect adult attention from the misbehavior. The bully might say: *We were just kidding. She knew it was a joke.*

When we work with younger children, we use a simplified definition of bullying:[7]

> **Bullying is when:**
>
> a stronger or more powerful person
>
> hurts or frightens
>
> a smaller or weaker person
>
> on purpose
>
> one time or more
>
> with unkind words, unfriendly touching,
>
> or by keeping them from having friends

Four Types of Bullying

There are four types of bullying: verbal, physical, relational, and cyberbullying. We've included examples of the forms bullying takes in older kids, as well as the "less mature" symptoms seen in younger kids. While it's hard to imagine young children experiencing the full-on cruelty and intense physicality of teen or adult bullying, the time to prevent that behavior is now, when children are little. We can put kids on another path while it's still easy (or, at least, easier).

1. **Verbal Bullying.** This is by far the most common type of bullying. It's everywhere. Boys and girls use it equally—adults, too. We've allowed it to become woven into our culture. Everyday insults, criticisms, rudeness, swearing, and putdowns are so common that we tune most of it out. Adults rarely intervene at this level. The problem with ignoring it is that we're creating a scaffold for the next level—even harsher verbal aggression, or the escalation to physical or relational bullying.

    Verbal bullying doesn't have to be complicated—one word will do: *Loser, Idiot, Baby,* or when they're older, *Fag, Gay,* or *Slut.* Being blown off with *Whatever.* Dismissive and cold, clearly sending the message *You're not one of us.* Verbal bullying can even be silent—with eye-rolling or the "L is for loser" sign. For younger kids who have not yet perfected the art of sarcasm, verbal bullying is usually loud and filled with insults.

2. **Physical Bullying.** This is the best-recognized form of bullying. We have long-standing mental images of physical bullying: a group of boys beating up another boy behind the school; a boy being pushed hard against, or completely into, a school locker; a boy's backpack ripped from his shoulder and the contents strewn on the floor or held up for display. We tend to think of physical bullying as boys' domain, and it's true that boys do more of it than girls, but girls, unfortunately, are catching up. Physical fights among girls are now common.

Adults intervene mostly commonly with physical bullying, but they usually get involved too late. Physical bullying, and even fights unrelated to bullying, develops over time. Adults monitoring the playground from a stationery viewpoint often miss the early signs. Adults can do a better job averting these problems by wandering around the playground, all through recess, watching and listening for incipient problems. Adults should wander around and listen for problems at home, too.

3. **Relational Bullying.** Relational bullying is the real or threatened social exclusion and isolation from former or current friends, or insurmountable barriers placed to prevent the establishment of new friendships. If boys are the primary physical aggressors, girls specialize in relational bullying.

    Relational bullying can take many forms, either behind a child's back or to her face: *You can't be our friend if you sit with Shawna, This table is just for 'The Populars'* (true story from a middle school!), *Do my math homework or I'll tell Jessie you said she's fat* (whether or not it was ever said), *You can't sit with us if you don't wear a skirt on Friday.* Girls have completely lost friendships over these issues. And it can happen in an instant: *When I went home from school on Friday, I had friends. I came back on Monday and I had no friends.*[8]

    What hurts so much about girls' relational bullying is the loss of friendships. Girls' friendships are based on close emotional connections, which are usually more important to girls than to boys, whose relationships tend to be more activity-based. Denying a girl access to a close, connected relationship with her peers can be devastating. Being obviously or covertly excluded from after-school and weekend social events, from everyday or special occasions, is really hurtful.

    While relational bullying peaks in middle school, "friendship hostage" situations are now occurring as early as Grade 1. Actually, first grade can be an especially rough year socially. Kids are just realizing that they're not exactly the same as their friends and that everybody doesn't always love everybody else. Kids start jockeying for friendships, sometimes using hurtful techniques they've learned from peers, older siblings, or TV shows.

    Grudge-holding magnifies girls' relationship problems. Real or imagined slights take on a life of their own—continuing for months or years, growing to larger circles of peers, and following a girl from year to year and from school to school.

4. **Cyberbullying** is an extension of relational bullying, but its technical complexity merits its own category. The ease of use and apparent anonymity online make it a compelling add-on to the other kinds of bullying. What begins in school as "old fashioned" girls' exclusion continues and escalates relentlessly, online and via cell phones, long after school has ended. Boys cyberbully, too, but unfortunately, girls are the "leaders" here.

    Cyberbullying is less of an issue in elementary school, but it's a growing problem with kids as young as 8 or 9, and certainly by age 10. It's important for parents of elementary school children to understand the "breadcrumb trail," the tiny, seemingly insignificant contributors—the little acts of meanness, the "cool" girls' circle that terrorizes other girls by withholding friendships, the verbal taunts *(Loser, Ugly, Nobody likes you),* smaller boys getting harassed and insulted while trying out for sports teams—a daily barrage of putdowns felt deeply by gentlehearted kids.

When kids don't understand where the behavioral limits are face-to-face, it will only get worse online, where inhibitions are minimized and there is no adult standing over the children's shoulders. This is NOT a case of *Boys will be boys* or *Girls will be girls.* **Adults must act now to stop this before it escalates—while our kids are still young, learning, and (at least occasionally) listening to us.**

Bullying peaks in middle school. Things typically calm down in high school as teens begin to settle into their sense of self, feel more secure and less vulnerable, and feel less driven to do mean things to other kids to ensure their own social standing.

High school has its own problems. Even though bullying frequency typically decreases in high school, what does occur can be extremely serious. "Payback" in the form of Columbine-style shootings usually happens in high school. Teens who've been taunted and victimized since elementary or middle school have much more free time in high school—with much less adult supervision. The Columbine rampage was meticulously planned on a website, a year before the shootings. Teens also have increased mobility and the money to turn their plans into reality. It's the perfect availability of resources for revenge for those who've waited years to get back at their tormentors. **The best time to stop these devastating high school tragedies is in elementary school—before they begin.**

Key Players in Bullying

There are three components to the bullying system:

1. Bully

2. Target

3. Bystanders

We have all played all three roles—bully, target, and, most frequently, bystander. While the bully and the target in kids' bullying are typically children, bystanders can be other children or adults, either of whom stand by and do nothing.

Efforts to decrease bullying must include attention to all three elements, with short- and long-term strategies for each. Bullying cannot be contained by focusing on one person or one piece of the system. It would be convenient if we could simply remove the bully, or send them out for remediation lessons, but even if that bully were to disappear, another would take their place. **Bullying only happens in environments (systems) that enable bullying, even if you can't see or don't understand how that is happening (yet). Unless you identify and correct ALL the factors that encourage, permit, and ignore bullying in your environment, it will continue to flourish and grow.**

What Bullying is NOT

- **Losing your temper and throwing a toy truck.** That's an overload behavior in an immature, developing brain. Young children often exhibit extreme behavior. This isn't bullying—it's poor social skills combined with a low boiling point. Meltdowns are a red flag for adults to monitor that child more closely, diverting him from the "tantrum on-ramp" long before the boiling point. Once the meltdown has started, it's too late for anything but damage control.

Adults can teach young children to "'use their words" to reduce frustration, along with simple stress management skills. Modeling good behavior for young children allows them to understand, when their brains mature, that the "why" of caring behavior reinforces the "how."

- **Teasing.** We use "teasing" to describe everything from good-natured, give-and-take banter between close friends to malicious, intentionally hurtful remarks to an overweight child about her body size or shape. For consistency and clarity, it's important to make a distinction between **teasing**, the acceptable, humor-based, equality-based version and **taunting**, the mean-spirited, one-sided, power-imbalanced bullying version. Renowned bullying prevention specialist Barbara Coloroso defines the differences as follows:[9]

Teasing	Taunting
- Roles can swap	- One-sided, power imbalance
- Not meant to hurt	- Intended to hurt
- Keeps dignity of all	- Humiliating, demeaning
- Kind and accepting	- Cruel, bigoted
- Only one part of relationship	- Major part of relationship
- Laughing *with* target	- Laughing *at* target
- Genuine humor in voice	- Sarcastic, makes excuses to divert adults: *We're just joking*
- No harm to self-esteem	- Harms self-esteem
- Stops when someone gets hurt or says *Stop*	- Continues, *especially* when target is upset or says *Stop*

The defining differences between teasing and taunting are:

- Can the roles reverse, or is the same child always being teased?

- Is the intent to hurt the target, either physically or emotionally?

- Is there humor on both sides?

- When the teasing goes too far—and it occasionally does—does the teaser back off and offer an apology, or does it intensify? If the teasing continues or intensifies, that's taunting, not teasing. Taunting is bullying; teasing is not.

- **Telling on Someone.** Kids have been taught to honor an imperfect code of silence: *Don't tell on your brother, Don't tell on your friend.* Then something dangerous happens and the first thing we ask is, *Why didn't you tell someone?* The culprit here is not the kids; rather, it's the language and the imprecise way we describe our value system. If we were clearer about which situations need an adult's help and gave kids more chances to practice, we'd get better results. Let's use Coloroso's distinction between tattling and telling:[10]

  - **Tattling** gets a child into trouble.

  - **Telling** gets a child out of trouble.

  Purposefully trying to get a kid into trouble can be bullying. Telling an adult when a kid needs help to get out of trouble can be lifesaving.

  Start when kids are young and use these words consistently to help them learn to tell the difference themselves. Ask and guide kids often and they will eventually internalize the difference. *Is that tattling or telling?* is a good question to ask a child because it puts the responsibility back on the child to reflect on both the seriousness of the problem and the underlying motivation behind the tattling or telling.

- **Conflict.** A big stumbling block to bullying prevention is the commonly misunderstood distinction between bullying and conflict and the frequent misapplication of conflict resolution tools or skills to solve a bullying issue. **You cannot use conflict resolution tools to solve bullying problems**. At best, this approach is ineffective. At worst, it can be explosive.

  For a while, adults labeled everything as a conflict. Now, too many problems get labeled as bullying. We need to understand the differences between them better in order to choose the best tools to solve each problem.

  Here are the main differences between bullying and conflict: Bullying is characterized by a persistent, one-way power imbalance with the power in the hands of the bully, who has the intent to harm the target. In contrast, **a conflict is between approximate equals.** The roles can reverse. An example of a simple conflict can be illustrated in a classroom that has only one computer. Let's say that today, Diego's on the computer and Amanda can't get on, even though she needs to finish her math challenge. It's a problem for Amanda today, but the situation could reverse if Amanda were to monopolize the computer tomorrow. The issue is between approximate equals, although Diego temporarily has control of a resource that Amanda needs.

  Conflicts are solved by negotiation. Negotiation involves compromise—each party gives up a little to create a solution where everybody benefits. *Let the kids work it out for themselves* is never a solution to bullying. No matter how skilled the kids are at conflict resolution, negotiation and compromise are not solutions to bullying and will not protect a child from further attacks.

Bullying is a complex topic, especially with the rapid evolution of issues, definitions, and technology. It's useful for adults to be mostly on the same page about the defining aspects of bullying. Now let's move forward toward solutions.

3

How Do I Help My Child Avoid Being a Target?

For Adults[11]

What Do Bullies Look for in Targets?

Kids who bully tend to pick on children who are—or appear to be—different. None of us want to think our child might attract the negative attention of a bully. There are, however, certain characteristics, behaviors, and personality traits that make it more likely a child will be targeted for bullying. A child who's noticeably different makes an easy target.

We firmly believe that each child's unique spirit and talents should be celebrated and encouraged. Making everyone "the same" is not the solution. In fact, it makes the problem worse. When everyone must conform to a small set of standard looks, behaviors, likes, and activities, it's far too easy to identify and bully any child who doesn't fit inside the box. What a boring world it would be if everyone looked and thought the same. Society loses, too, if the independent ideas of future visionaries, creative thinkers, and leaders are stamped out.

Every child—and perhaps *especially* those who are unique or stand out the most—will benefit from learning a basic set of social skills to ease their interactions and improve friendships with peers, older and younger kids, and adults. These skills will help a child feel comfortable joining a new class, group, school, sport, or activity; being a guest at another child's home; or embracing the adventures and uncertainties of travel. It's about finding the right balance—maintaining a child's unique individuality while helping them learn social skills that will enable them to fit in with their peers. **That's why it's just as important to help kids make friends as it is to help them avoid being bullied.**

Most risk factors for bullying can be minimized and managed by alert and caring adults who intervene at the earliest signs. Prevention is much easier—and more effective—than trying to repair a situation gone wrong. This book will help you guide your child toward positive and protective skills and behaviors.

Adults must set the big-picture framework for kids' behavior. Grown-ups need to communicate their values to kids, creating safe and welcoming homes, schools, and communities where kids are respected and accepted, even when a child's behavior needs some improvement. Standards and boundaries for acceptable behavior between kids must be established. When adults are clear and consistent, kids will eventually internalize the rules for respectful behavior, reducing (but not eliminating) the need for adult monitoring.

What if My Child is the Bully?

You may be reading this with a nagging worry: *"Could my child be the one acting like a bully?"* Most of us have had that thought cross our minds, even briefly. It's completely normal. All children can—and most do—slip into bullying behavior, especially when they're young (or teens) and "trying on" different roles and behaviors. Kids who have been targets may act as bullies in other settings. Testing the limits is a child's job. It's *our* job, as adults, to monitor their behavior and gently guide kids back into mostly kind-hearted, empathic, supportive behavior towards others.

Parents must be willing to look bravely at our children's behavior and assess *and accept* if our child is acting overly aggressive. *"Boys will be boys"* or *"Girls will be girls"* is not the right call when kids are being hurt. Time to step in, restate the standards and boundaries and be clear about the behavior we expect to see. Mistakes will be made. We must be strong and teach our children the strength of ownership, apology, and repair.

Creating a culture of kindness starts with adults. We're the role models and our behavior speaks louder than our words. Adults aren't perfect, but we must look with an honest eye at whether our behavior measures up

to the respectful standards we're setting for kids. Do we gossip on the phone while our child overhears? Do many shows we watch feature bullying and humiliation? Do bullies rule our workplaces? When adults talk and complain about workplace bullying—without solving the problem—and when kids see it on TV, kids learn that bullying is an expected and accepted part of adult life. It's a big project to clean up our workplaces, but adults must act authentically to be credible mentors and guides to kids.

The rest of this book will: (1) Identify common problem areas for kids that can make them vulnerable to bullying and (2) Provide some solutions and skills to work on with your child. Every child is different, with unique strengths and weaknesses, and develops social skills and emotional intelligence at different times. Start by choosing one or two areas that fit your child's current needs. Ask for suggestions from your child's teachers—they spend a lot of time observing your child in action.

Let us be extremely clear: It is the responsibility of **adults** to monitor for, identify, and protect children from bullying. The life-long, confidence-boosting skills we are teaching kids with this book will help them speak up, make friends, and protect others, but this does not remove or diminish the ultimate adult responsibility for children's bullying prevention—at home, at school, and in the community.

Have patience. These new skills take months to learn, not minutes. Look for opportunities to reinforce them in situations that occur in your child's everyday life. Ask your child's teacher for support.

Teachers: When you're using this book in your classroom, ask parents to reinforce the concepts of kindness, respect, and empathy. Send newsletters home describing how the class has created a climate of caring. Include an activity from Chapter 5 for parents and children to do together. All adults musts pay attention to ensure we create environments where children are accepted as individuals and treated with respect.

Mostly, relax and enjoy the process of learning and working with your child or class. As a parent or teacher, it's heartwarming to see children develop and use new skills. Being tense, even when the stakes are high, reduces your chances for success and growth. Make it a fun experiment. Let us know which ideas worked best and how you customized and we'll share it with our network!

Common Problems That Make Kids Vulnerable to Bullying

- **Problem: Your child is new to the school, community, or country**. New kids tend to have fewer friends and be less "embedded" in the school community (they lack multiple, strong relationships). There's often a language barrier, too.

- **Solution: Adults must set the tone, connecting the newcomer to rotating "buddies" or "ambassadors" for the first 2–3 months** (yes, months). With adult supervision, peers can be assigned to help the new child find her way around school. Ask the teacher to introduce her to peers and adults in the school, tell her about school rules and procedures, and facilitate her inclusion at lunch, recess, and other in- and after-school social activities. Having someone to sit with eases entry into the social system. Invite your child's classmates to your home for after-school activities. Ask the teacher to identify kids who walk home on the same route or travel on the same bus and can walk or sit with your child. We'll talk about this in more depth in Chapter 5.

- **Problem: Children who are different in some way, including:**

  - **Age:** Old or young for their grade.

  - **Size:** Big or small, thin or overweight. Overweight kids are disproportionately targeted.[12]

  - **Disabilities:** Especially physical or observable disabilities.

  - **Intellectual differences:** Learning disabled or gifted (especially once labeled by the school), or gifted + learning disabled (these characteristics often coexist, making a child doubly vulnerable to bullying).

  - **LGBT:** As kids become aware of their sexuality and sexual orientation, kids who are—or suspect they may be—LGBT kids experience a significantly greater risk of being bullied.[13]

- **Solution: Adults must take the lead, clearly stating and demonstrating that we accept everyone's differences.** Some strengths and weaknesses are more visible than others. We should be able to get support when we need it and give support when we can. Adults must monitor kids' social interactions closely, catching mistakes and missteps. Kids need to know we mean it—nobody should be left out or excluded.

- **Problem: Insecure body language.** When a child has insecure body language, he looks vulnerable—like an easy target.

- **Solution: Teach stronger, more positive body language.** Demonstrate good posture—how to make direct eye contact, smile, walk, and move with confidence.

- **Problem: Lack of or awkward social skills.** Kids acquire smooth social skills at different ages. Some are socially comfortable at amazingly young ages; many are still awkward in high school. Many adults have not fully acquired graceful social skills either!

- **Solution: Help your child learn the skills of friendship.** For kids lacking social finesse, parents and teachers can teach some useful skills: how to make friends, how to maintain friendships, how to "break the ice" when entering an established group, how to tell a joke, etc. Adults can share tips that will help a kid feel more socially confident and secure.

  Teach your child to be a good friend. Help her learn to become a good listener, ask questions to draw out conversation, be friendly and helpful, and avoid gossiping. Coach your child to respect physical boundaries (keep her hands to herself, be aware of other people's personal space, don't stand too close or laugh too loud in someone's face, and learn to read body language so she'll know if she's bothering someone).[14] Point out good and bad friendship skills on TV. For a list of our favorite books about friendship for younger children, see Chapter 5, Activity 7.

- **Problem: Cultural Differences**. Taunting because of cultural differences still occurs and has increased since the September 11, 2001, US terrorist attacks. Sometimes the taunting is overt, but more likely, it is covert: *Your lunch smells funny* or *What's in your hair?* (said with a sneer, not curiosity).

- **Solution: Create environments where we—and our kids—celebrate diversity and learn about one another's different backgrounds**. Multicultural lunches or dinners, where students and their families bring food to school for all to share (always be careful about allergies), can showcase the varying ways different cultures might use the same ingredient, for example.

- **Problem: Poor choice of friends.** Friendships should be grounded in respect for self and for others. Picking the right friends is a key life skill, but it's difficult at every age. Does your child's friend put him down, embarrass him in front of other friends, or talk about him behind his back?

- **Solution: Teach your child the qualities of respectful friendship—how to be a good friend and how to recognize good and bad friends and friendships.** Kids with respect for self and for others don't act like bullies, don't choose friends who act like bullies, and don't stand by while others are bullied. Role play with your child, demonstrating what respectful friendships look like. Help your child be alert to the warning signs of toxic or disrespectful friendships at all ages. (We know you can hardly imagine this now, but you'll really be glad your kids have learned to avoid toxic relationships in the dating years. You can thank us later!)

- **Problem: Specific personality factors**. Kids with certain personality traits are more vulnerable to being bullied. These include:

  - **Sensitive**: Bullies know how to bait and get a rise out of these kids.

  - **Submissive**: Kids who act like bullies won't find much resistance here.

  - **Aggressive**: These kids are often hyper-reactive. Like sensitive children, they can be easily baited and upset, which can be endlessly "entertaining" to others.

  - **Annoying**: Provocative targets get little sympathy or empathy from their peers, teachers, and school officials. Adults and peers often say these kids "bring it on themselves." Provocative targets do not deserve to be bullied. What they need is protection and help to learn better social skills.

  - **Introverted**: Shy kids often have few friends and keep to themselves. Not well-embedded in the social structure, they make easy targets, especially when walking alone between classes, or after school.

- **Solution: Adults must take the lead to make sure that children with challenging personality traits are not targeted. In addition, these children need specific social skills training**. Sensitive kids can be taught to develop a thicker skin, learning how to distinguish kindhearted teasing from mean-spirited taunting, how to banter and exchange jokes, and how to engage in age-appropriate social conversation. Submissive kids can learn to be more assertive. Aggressive kids will benefit from activities to help them find their gentler sides. Provocative targets need a chance to practice and learn social skills to soften their rough edges (start with one behavior at a time). Introverts (and extroverts) need help learning to moderate their levels of introversion (or extroversion) in each situation.

- **Problem: Your child has a conflict with another child, or group of kids, at school.**

- **STOP & CHECK: First, ensure that your child is safe and that this is a conflict, not bullying. If you have concerns for your child's safety, immediately enlist the help of the school staff.** Once you're sure it's a conflict and there's no safety issue, proceed with this solution.

- **Solution:** Make the teacher or another adult aware of the issue and ask for extra supervision to diffuse and solve the problem. **DON'T ask for your child to be separated or isolated from the other children.** Give your child the chance to learn how to work with others who have different work ethics, abilities, and opinions, and to learn the valuable life skills of compromise and negotiation. We often don't have a choice of whom to work with at school or at work. The earlier we learn to work with a wide range of people—and learn how to pick good friends and working partners—the better.

  Parents often ask if they should directly contact the parents of the other children in the conflict. In general, we recommend you don't approach them directly, especially if the problem involves bullying. More on this later when we discuss additional tips for handling bullying situations in Chapter 5, Activity 10.

- **Problem: Your child doesn't like everyone in his class.**

- **Solution: There's no solution, because this isn't really a problem.** He doesn't have to like everyone in the class. He doesn't have to be best friends with everyone, either. Best friends or not, everyone in the class must be treated with kindness and respect. Encourage and reward positive, accepting, and inclusive behavior!

- **Problem: Your child has bad manners or poor personal hygiene.** This can cause other kids and adults to avoid or make fun of your child.

- **Solution: Teach your child to be clean and have good manners.** Being aware of hair, fingernails, teeth/breath, nose, and armpits is a necessary skill! Work on good table manners: mouth closed when chewing, use a napkin, no burping noises (or say *Excuse me*), etc. Help your child learn how to be a comfortable guest at someone else's house. Teach kids to say *Please* and *Thank you* and to help clean up after a meal. Kids will learn quickly that their manners around other kids can be more relaxed than around adults.

- **Problem: Kids with certain disabilities, like Autism Spectrum Disorder (ASD), are uniquely vulnerable to bullying because of their lack of social skills**. Unable to read social cues from faces or body language, and often very slow to learn these cues—even with adult support—these kids are easily subjected to the same "joke" again and again.

- **Solution: Adults need to step in and insist that kids help others who don't have their same skills**. Then we must monitor and follow-up to make sure classmates are providing positive support, as well as not treating these kids as targets. This kind of adult and peer support also applies to the earlier discussion of kids with other learning disabilities.

  Although it can take a long time to train kids with ASD or other disorders to recognize facial expressions and social cues, it's worth the effort. Many kids can really improve their perceptions or develop an internal flowchart to help protect themselves from harm or humiliation: *If I see this expression* <a sneer>, *then it might mean this* <they're taunting me>, *and I should try to do this* <walk away or go to another friend>. Rotating buddy systems will help protect these children, too.[15]

- **Problem: Your child says she's being teased because she doesn't have cool clothes.**

- **Solution: Kids are actually protected from bullying and more likely to fit in when they have some of the same clothing and accessories as their peer group.** Help your child fit in with their clothing choices, but membership in a group of friends shouldn't have to be bought with a $200 pair of sneakers.

  Clothing doesn't need to be new, but it should be clean and sized appropriately for your child—pants, shirts, and sweaters should not be too long or short. Take some time to learn about current age-appropriate fashion trends. Follow some—but not all—of the trends in her peer group. Help your child fit in without being a fashion victim, crossing the line into inappropriate clothing, or emptying your wallet. Find a good balance.

- **Problem: Your child only has one friend**. Kids who act like bullies tend to pick on kids who are quiet, isolated, and have few friends.

- **Solution: Help your child make more friends**. Having even one friend can protect your child's self-esteem and be tremendously insulating against bullying. Having a few more friends is even better, providing deeper connections to the school social scene and making it likely your child always has someone to hang out with, even if his one best friend isn't there.

  Respect your child's basic personality while encouraging him to grow. Introverts will naturally be happy with fewer friends; extroverts typically want more. Talk with your child about how to make more friends—one friend at a time. Invite individual children from your child's class to play at your home or go to the park with you. When children get to know each other individually, outside of school, in-school bullying is diminished.

- **Problem: Your child has only one group of friends (belongs to only one social circle)**. It's all good until that group starts having friendship troubles. Then what does your child do?

- **Solution**: **Encourage your child to make friendships with kids from several social groups**. The more respectful friendships your child has, the more embedded she will be in the social system of every group she belongs to, and the less likely she will be bullied. It's fine to have preferred friends, but having friends in multiple social groups will help your child be more resilient to problems occurring in any particular group.

  This social cushion is especially valuable for girls during those frenemy-filled years of late elementary and middle school. When things get tense within your child's only group of friends, it can feel like social disaster. When she has friendships with several groups, if there's a problem with one group of friends, she can slide over to another group. Building friendships in several environments encourages resilience.

  Schools can do their part to soften the boundaries between social groups by having activities such as: (1) sitting with different kids one day a week at lunch, (2) pairing kids as reading buddies, or creating similar opportunities for older students to help younger students, (3) sharing school newsletter interviews of new students, celebrating students' special accomplishments, etc. With these activities, schools can lessen the influence of cliques and make it much easier for kids to move back and forth between social groups.

4

What Kids Need to Know About Bullying

For Adults & Kids

How to Use This Chapter

This section is written for kids and contains important information about finding friends and avoiding bullies. Three short stories are included to enhance these concepts. Parents, read this chapter with your children. The STOP AND THINK sections will help you guide your child in thought-provoking discussions about the characters and their actions. The first story, *Addy's Playdate Surprise*, is for children 5–6. The second story, *The Alien from Planet PawPaw*, is geared toward kids 7–8. The third, *Tyler Stands Up for a Friend*, is targeted at children 9–10.

Feel free to modify the material depending on the child's or student's age, reading ability, and the type of bullying or friendship problems you're experiencing or trying to prevent.

Don't assume a story is too "young" for a certain age group. Perhaps surprisingly, it's often better to use simple stories geared to younger children to illustrate specific lessons. Complex stories, although interesting to older kids, can confuse or distract from the lesson you're trying to teach.

Don't assume a story is too "old," either. For pre-literate children, read the story yourself first, then tell them a simplified version that still covers the main points.

If your child has the reading ability, let her read it to you, or kids can take turns reading aloud in class. It's an opportunity to practice reading, demonstrate emotion, and learn new vocabulary!

Have fun!

Welcome to Kids!

For Adults & Kids

It's Back-to-School Time!

Wait! Is summer over already? It went so fast! I don't want to go back to school yet! Did you know that many kids feel this way? To be fair, there are some really great things about starting a new school year. You'll learn something new every day in school. You might become a better reader, writer, artist, or musician. You can learn to speak Spanish, French, or Mandarin. You'll explore Math, Science, Social Studies, and many other subjects.

It's fun to gather your school supplies for the new year. Maybe you'll be in a new classroom. You might be in a new school, or a different part of your old school. You could have a cubby or locker for the first time. Maybe you'll get assigned to your own desk!

Some kids look forward to seeing their friends from last year or friends from their neighborhood. Other kids can't wait to take the bus by themselves.

Even with all the exciting things to look forward to, some kids are a little nervous about going back to school: *What if I don't know anyone? Will anyone sit with me at lunch? Will I have friends to play with at recess? What if my friends from last year aren't in my class this year?*

Some kids are more than a little nervous about the new school year—they're downright scared: *Will that kid who was mean to me last year be in my class this year? Will my friend's older brother pick on me on the playground? What if the tough kids in gym class make fun of me again this year?*

Guess what? It's perfectly normal to be a little nervous. You're probably having the same thoughts as many of your classmates. If you're *more* than a little nervous, you should talk to someone who can help: your mom or dad, grandparent, older brother or sister, your favorite teacher, or your guidance counselor. If you're worried about being bullied, please let a grown-up know so that, together, you can make a plan to prevent it from happening. Everyone deserves to feel safe at school and while traveling to and from school.

Start the year with a smile! A smile sends the message that you're friendly. Make friends with kids who are nice to you and nice to others. Get involved in activities outside of school, too! Soccer, baseball, karate, ballet—whatever interests you. Find friends who like those hobbies, too.

You are a good person, and you deserve to be treated with kindness and respect. Read this book with your mom or dad (or both), your grandparent, or caregiver to learn some tips that will help you make good friends and avoid bullies.

Have a great year in school!

Him or Her?

You will notice that when we talk about kids, sometimes we use "him" and sometimes we use "her." We do this on purpose so you will remember that kids who act like bullies can be either boys or girls. Children who get picked on can also be boys or girls. Whether we use "him" or "her" in a sentence, we are really talking about both boys and girls.

We know that kids who act like bullies can change their behavior. So can kids who are targets. That is why we try—and we ask you to try—not to label any kid as a "bully" or a "target." Instead of saying, *Will's a bully,* try saying, *Will acted like a bully when he pushed me.* We will still use the words "bully" and "target" to explain these ideas to you, but we're not calling any children by those names.

Making Friends

Whether you have lots of friends or only one or two, it's important to find other kids who share your interests. Find friends who like the same sports, video games, cartoons, or books as you do. When you talk to a new person, you're sure to find something in common. Maybe you both have older or younger brothers and sisters. Look for friends who are kind and accept you as you are.

If a friend constantly says mean things to you, makes fun of you or other people, hurts your feelings, breaks rules, or puts you in uncomfortable situations, sometimes you can get him to stop by telling him how you feel. Sometimes you will have to find other friends who treat you nicely. Friendship takes work. Friends stick up for one another and care about each other's feelings.

The stories and ideas in this chapter are about how kids can prevent and deal with bullying. Read the stories to your parent, if you can. Ask for help with any words or ideas you don't understand.

How Can I Avoid Being a Target of Bullying?

Many kids who get picked on think that it happens because they are doing something wrong. Most of the time, that's just not true. Kids who act like bullies look for targets with very specific characteristics. Why? Bullies like to feel they are more powerful than their targets. That's why bullies often  pick on kids who are smaller, weaker, younger, or different from other kids in some way. They're looking for someone who will be hurt or upset by what they say or do— and who won't fight back.

The top three things that bullies look for in a target are:

1. Someone who is different in some way.

2. Someone who can be made to feel bad about herself.

3. Someone who doesn't have any friends or is alone most of the time.

Can I Be Different & Not Be Bullied?

Yes, you can. Bullies often don't understand that everyone is unique and that we should be proud of that. We all have different heights, weights, skin colors, and face and body features. Some of us are good at sports, while others are good at dancing, drawing, or playing chess. School is easy for some people, while others must work hard to learn new things.

These differences are what make the world interesting. Be proud of what makes you different from other kids! Find friends who share or accept your differences. If you come from another culture, teach friends and classmates about your language, food, unique clothing, or country. Ask parents and teachers for help making new friends. If you are a target of bullying, tell your parent or teacher (or another adult that you trust) so they can help you.

People are most comfortable with what's familiar to them. Adjusting to something new means changing the way you look, act, or think. Some of us are better at adjusting to new things than others. Bullies are generally not good at changing the way they think about people who are different from them, but we can help them change.

Help! I Don't Want to Be a Target!

The first thing you should do when someone says or does something mean to you is say to yourself, ***I am a good person, and I deserve to be treated with kindness and respect.*** Memorize this sentence. Say it over and over, to yourself and out loud. It may feel funny to say this sentence at first, but it's really important that you believe these words! Everyone deserves to be treated with kindness and respect. People who act like bullies try to make you forget this.

Next, look the kid who said or did something mean in the eyes and say in a calm but firm voice, ***What you did (or what you said) really hurt my feelings, and I don't like that.*** Stand up straight with your shoulders back, but don't yell or scream. This step is designed to give the kid who said or did something mean a chance to realize her mistake and apologize.

Maybe there was a misunderstanding. If that kid does not apologize after you make your feelings known, or she says something worse, you can either walk away without saying anything, or say, *I'll come back and play when you speak to me nicely.* Let a grown-up know that you tried to deal with the mean behavior, but you need some help. Even if you ask for help, you are standing up for yourself by letting the kid who said or did something mean to you know that her behavior is not OK. Everyone deserves to be treated with kindness and respect. Never let someone acting like a bully make you feel bad about yourself.

Help! I Don't Want to Feel Alone

Whenever someone makes us feel hurt, sad, insecure, or uncomfortable by commenting on the way we look, act, or think, our first reaction might be to go off and be alone to get away from the bad feelings. Sometimes a little "alone time" can help clear our heads, but too much can make us feel really lonely. Even kids in the most popular groups feel lonely sometimes. Some people who are really famous today—singers, actors, or sports heroes—were bullied a lot as kids because they were different. You're not alone! Bullying is wrong—even if it happens often. Adults are working to change this, and we need your help!

The problem with being alone is that you can become be an easy target for kids who act like bullies. **Bullies want power, and it's easier to bully one person than it is to bully a group.**

The best way to stop a bullying attack is for a group of kids to stand up and protect the target. We call that being an **upstander**. If even one other kid acts like an upstander, there is a good chance the bullying will stop—even without a grown-up's help. Kids have the power!

One of the most important things to know is: Who's got your back—your friends, parents, teachers, or counselors? Who can you count on for help when you need it? Whose back do you have? That's good to know, too.

How Can I Build an Anti-Target Shield?

It's a good idea to have friends inside AND outside of school. Find friends through sports, hobbies, your church or synagogue or mosque, your neighborhood community center, or camp. Find out about clubs and after-school activities in your neighborhood. Ask your parents to help you arrange playdates and sleepovers with kids with common interests. Get to know your classmates outside of school. Don't forget that you can be friends with boys *and* girls. You don't have to "like, like" each other as a boyfriend or girlfriend—you can just be friends.

An important safety tip: If you are having a problem with someone who is acting like a bully, don't put yourself in danger. Think about your traveling routes and make sure you are not alone. Sit with someone on the bus or walk with someone to and from the bus stop and around school. Know where teachers and other grown-ups can be found if you need help. Don't be left alone in locker rooms or on playgrounds. Pay attention to your surroundings and tell a grown-up if you EVER feel unsafe in any way.

Let's go back and reread the first two sentences of this chapter: Many kids who get picked on think that it happens because they are doing something wrong. Most of the time, that's just not true.

Did you notice that we said, MOST of the time, that's just not true? Here's something to think about: Sometimes a kid might behave in ways that make it more likely that someone might bully him. It's not right or fair, but it does happen. If a kid is really sensitive, or loses his temper easily, someone might pick on that kid because they know he can be easily pushed to put on a "show." If a bully knows he can't upset you, he'll be less interested in picking on you.

Sometimes targets get tired of hearing mean comments, or getting pushed around, and strike back with their own comments or punches. This can turn into a BIG problem. Even if it seems fair for a target to strike back at bullying behavior, it's never a good idea. Two wrongs don't make a right.

Targets never deserve to be bullied, but we should all be aware of how our behavior affects others. We must keep our hands to ourselves, respect one another's personal space, and learn to notice body language and facial expressions when working or playing with others.

Something that might seem like fun teasing to one person might annoy or hurt another. If someone tells you that your behavior is hurting her feelings or making her uncomfortable, that behavior must stop immediately—even if it was not intentional —and *especially* if it was.

Keep these ideas in mind and your anti-target shield will be ready for action!

Addy's Playdate Surprise

For Adults & Kids

One Saturday morning in late August, Addy's mom invited a girl named Maya to their house for a playdate. Maya and her family had just moved to Addy's neighborhood, and Addy's mom thought it would be nice for the girls to get to know each other before school started, because they would be in the same class. Addy was excited to meet someone new. She hoped Maya liked to play with dolls and stuffed animals.

Maya rang the doorbell. Addy's mom opened the door and said, *Maya! It's so nice to meet you! My name is Mrs. Thomas and this is my daughter, Addy. She is six years old, just like you.*

Hi, Maya said, smiling shyly.

Let's go play in my room! said Addy.

I'll make lunch in about 30 minutes, said Mrs. Thomas. *Enjoy yourselves, girls!*

Addy ran up the steps and Maya followed her into a bright pink room. Dolls and toys were scattered all over the floor, and a beautiful dollhouse stood next to the bed. Maya sat on the floor and picked up Addy's favorite doll.

Her name's Sarah, Addy said proudly.

Only babies play with dolls, said Maya.

I'm not a baby, said Addy, shocked by what Maya said.

Why is your room so pink? asked Maya, sneering.

Because pink is my favorite color, answered Addy.

Purple's a better color than pink. This room looks stupid, said Maya. *I don't want to play with someone who likes pink and plays with dolls.*

Addy didn't know what to do. Maya was really hurting her feelings. Should she say something mean back to Maya? Should she go and get her mom? Was Maya right? Was purple better than pink? Were dolls just for babies?

STOP & THINK

Parents: Ask your child what she would do if Maya said those mean things to her.

Remind your child that it's OK for people to like different things, and friends should respect each other's choices. Stress that it's not a good solution to be mean to someone who's acting like a bully. Let your child know that she can always come to you for help and that you'll always have her back.

Addy felt her eyes start to tear up. Then she remembered something she learned in kindergarten last year. Her teacher, Miss Plum, told the class that all people are different and that it's OK to like different things. She also taught them that if anyone ever said or did something mean to them, the first thing they should say to themselves is, *I am a good person, and I deserve to be treated with kindness and respect.* That means that everyone deserves to be treated nicely and everyone's feelings are important. Quietly, Addy repeated the sentence to herself two times. She felt a little bit better.

Do you like checkers? Addy asked hopefully.

No, I don't like checkers. I don't like your room. And I don't like you! screamed Maya.

Addy felt awful! Why was Maya being so mean? Addy stood up and pushed her shoulders back. She looked right at Maya and said: *You really hurt my feelings with all of the mean things you said, and I don't like that. I am going to go get my mom to tell her that I don't want to play with you until you can treat me nicely.* She turned and walked toward the door.

Wait, said Maya. *Please wait.* Maya burst into tears. Addy walked back over to where Maya was sitting on the floor.

I'm sorry, sobbed Maya. *I'm just so sad. And I'm mad! I didn't want to move. I had to leave all my friends and I have no friends here. What if no one likes me at my new school? What if I don't know where to go? Sorry I was so mean, but I feel like I don't like anything about being here.* She wiped her nose on her sleeve.

It's OK, Maya. I'll be your friend, and I'll show you where to go in school. There are lots of nice kids in our class. Addy put her hand on Maya's shoulder.

Just then, Addy's mom called upstairs: *Girls, lunch is ready!* Addy gave Maya a tissue to wipe her eyes.

Maya said, *Thanks, Addy. I'm glad we'll be friends.* Addy scooped up her doll and gave another doll to Maya. The new friends went downstairs to have lunch. As they ate their grilled cheese sandwiches, Addy told Maya all about the kids in their class.

STOP & THINK

Parents: Talk to your child about Maya's behavior. How did it make Addy feel? Even though there is never an excuse for acting mean towards another person, sometimes it helps to understand why it might be happening. Thinking about another person's feelings (both the target's and the bully's) will help your child to develop empathy and the skills to resolve conflicts between friends. Review how Addy did not let Maya's comments shake her confidence in her own choices. Discuss how Addy calmly and firmly stood up for herself.

The Alien from Planet PawPaw

For Adults & Kids

One day, an alien from planet PawPaw landed in the middle of a school playground on Earth. The alien's name was Mergg. He looked very much like a human kid—except that he had spiky, green hair and gray skin. The students on the playground ran over to meet Mergg and see his cool spaceship. Most of the kids were friendly and asked Mergg where he came from and what it was like to drive a spaceship. Jackson, a tall, tough 6th grader who always acted like a bully, pushed his way through the crowd to stand next to Mergg.

Hey, why is your hair so weird? Jackson asked, as he stared down at Mergg.

Hi, Mergg replied nervously. *My name is Mergg, and I'm from planet PawPaw. What's your name?*

A few more students gathered around the boys to see if there would be a fight. Jackson always started fights with kids who were just minding their own business.

I asked you a question, sneered Jackson. *Why is your hair so weird? Did someone sneeze on your head?*

Some of the students giggled. Some looked scared. Some walked away. Mergg didn't know what to say. He looked at the other kids. No one else had spiky, lime-colored locks. Suddenly, he felt embarrassed because he was different. Mergg blushed, his shoulders drooped, and he looked down at the ground.

STOP & THINK

Parents: Jackson acted like a bully toward Mergg. Make it clear to your child that this was not Mergg's fault; Mergg did nothing wrong. Bullying affects kids of all ages, and we want to teach our kids to make themselves as "bully-proof" as possible. Ask your child what factors made Mergg a target? Why was he more likely to be picked on by a bully like Jackson?

Mergg was more likely to be picked on because he was the only one on the playground with green hair and gray skin, making him *different* from the other kids. Also, because Mergg had just landed on Earth, he didn't have many friends yet. Kids who act like bullies tend to seek out kids who are alone. Finally, Jackson was able to make Mergg feel bad about himself. Mergg's body language (he blushed, his shoulders drooped, and he looked down at the ground) showed that Mergg was self-conscious about his hair, and this gave Jackson a sense of power. Bullies love to feel that sense of power.

Jackson saw that he was making Mergg uncomfortable. He puffed up his chest and shoved Mergg to the ground.

Are all the green-haired freaks from your planet such wimps? Jackson asked, looking down at Mergg. *Why don't you get back in that tin can of a spaceship and go home!*

Jackson received high-fives from two of his friends. The other kids were silent. Some of them looked shocked. A girl named Annie ran away. Mergg rubbed his elbow as a tear slid down his cheek. Just then, the doors to the gymnasium opened and a group of 8th graders scrambled on to the playground. As Jackson leaned over to flick at Mergg's hair, an 8th grader named Max walked over to the group.

What's going on here? asked Max.

I'm protecting our playground from green-haired freaks! replied Jackson.

Are you acting like a bully again, Jackson? asked Max, who was bigger and taller than Jackson. *You act tough, but you always pick on kids who are younger and smaller than you. Leave this kid alone!*

Max extended his hand toward Mergg and helped him up. A few of the kids in the circle went to stand behind Mergg.

As Max walked away, he looked back at Mergg and said, *By the way, cool hair, dude!*

Jackson looked flustered for a moment, but then the sneer returned to his face. He moved toward Mergg again.

Now, there's no one to stick up for you, creep, said Jackson.

But something had changed. The kids who had moved to stand behind Mergg now moved between Mergg and Jackson and crossed their arms in front of their chests.

You heard Max, said a boy named Chen. *Stop acting like a bully, Jackson.*

Shut up, Chen, yelled Jackson. *Mergg is a freak. Do you see anyone else with such wacky hair? He doesn't belong here.* Jackson was now staring at Chen, and Chen nervously wondered if maybe he shouldn't have said anything. To his surprise, other kids started to speak up.

Back off, Jackson, said another boy named Carlos. *Mergg didn't do anything to you. Stop picking on him!*

We're all different, said a short girl named Lisa. *I think Mergg's hair looks awesome!* She reached up and put her hand on Mergg's shoulder.

Jackson scowled. He realized he couldn't act like a bully against a whole group of kids. He walked away with the two kids who had laughed with him while he picked on Mergg.

Mergg looked at his new friends and smiled. He thanked them for sticking up for him. Just then, Annie returned to the group with a tall, thin teacher named Mr. Wigglesworth.

When I saw Jackson push Mergg, I ran to find a grown-up, Annie said as she caught her breath.

STOP & THINK

Parents: Help your child identify the story characters who acted like upstanders. Who acted like bystanders?

Annie was the first kid who acted like an upstander; though it may have appeared that she ran away when Jackson pushed Mergg to the ground, she actually went to get help from a grown-up. Max acted like an upstander when he confronted Jackson and told him to stop picking on Mergg. Remind your child that safety should always be considered when confronting a bully. There are many ways to support a target that do not involve directly confronting a bully. Sometimes, kids can act like upstanders through their body language and actions. All of the characters in the story who stood around Mergg with their arms crossed in a message of protection were upstanders. Chen and Carlos became upstanders when they stood up to Jackson and told him to stop picking on Mergg. Lisa was an upstander when she reminded the group that they were all unique. She also said she liked Mergg's hair color—even if it was different.

Jackson's friends were bystanders. They did nothing to help Mergg while Jackson was picking on him. They even laughed at Jackson's taunting remarks. Remind your child that anyone who stands by and does nothing to help someone who is being bullied is acting like a bystander. Encourage your child to become an upstander.

Is everything OK here? asked Mr. Wigglesworth.

It is now, replied Carlos. *We stopped someone from acting like a bully by sticking together and standing up for our new friend, Mergg.*

Excellent! exclaimed Mr. Wigglesworth. *I'm very proud of you. You must be Mergg,* said Mr. Wigglesworth as he extended one hand and pushed his glasses up on his nose with the other. *I am the 4th grade science teacher. Are you a new student?*

Nice to meet you, said Mergg. *I'm from planet PawPaw, and I'm visiting Earth today.*

This is so exciting! exclaimed Mr. Wigglesworth. *We have so many questions for you! Would you like to come to my classroom and tell us all about your planet? May I see your spaceship? Is PawPaw in our Solar System? How many aliens live on PawPaw? Is there life on other planets? How much fuel did it take to get here?*

Mr. Wigglesworth asked about 20 more questions in a row without waiting for a single answer. Mergg smiled as he followed his new friends into the science classroom. It was going to be a fun afternoon!

STOP & THINK

Parents: Ask your child to name three kids she thinks are good friends. Does your child think these kids would stand up for her if she were ever picked on? Would she stand up for them as well?

4.4

Tyler Stands Up for a Friend

For Adults & Kids

Tyler jumped down from his front porch and sat in the grass to tie his sneakers. Later today, he was planning to try out for the second base position on his school's Little League baseball team. He'd been practicing all summer with Rico, a boy whose family moved into the house across the street in June.

Rico was 10, the same age as Tyler, and they had become good friends right away. They both liked video games, comic books, and hamburgers without cheese. They both had annoying younger sisters and loved baseball. When they weren't playing catch or practicing batting in one of their backyards, they were watching baseball games on TV. Tyler's mom called them "the baseball twins," which was funny because they looked nothing alike. Tyler was tall for his age, with broad shoulders and big muscles in his  arms and legs. He had curly brown hair and large brown eyes. Rico was short and very thin. He had straight black shoulder-length hair that he often pulled into a ponytail.

As Tyler finished tying his shoes, Rico slammed his front door and ran across the street carrying his bat and glove. Tyler picked up his own gear and met Rico on the sidewalk. As they walked to the park, Rico told Tyler that he was nervous about trying out for the team today.

You have nothing to worry about, Rico, said Tyler. He leaned toward Rico and nudged his shoulder. *You can catch anything, and I know Coach will want you to play on the team.*

Thanks, said Rico. *I hope I don't drop the ball because I'm nervous.*

We'll have time to warm up before tryouts. Just pretend we're in my backyard throwing the ball around, said Tyler.

Rico was quiet and looked at the ground. *I'm not just nervous about the tryouts. Some of the kids from my old school used to pick on me because I'm so small,* Rico said quietly. *They were really mean. They called me names and pushed me into the lockers all the time. I was scared to go to school some days.*

Tyler had never been the target of bullying. He wondered what it would be like to be scared to go to school or be picked on because of the way he looked.

STOP & THINK

Parents: Ask your child if he has ever been picked on. Has he ever had a friend who was picked on? How did your child handle the situation? Remind him that he is a good person, and he deserves to be treated with kindness and respect. Also remind your child that he can always come to you for help, and that you will always have his back.

As the boys reached the park, Tyler was thinking about what to say to Rico when Coach called out, *Hey, Tyler! Get your butt over here. We're waiting for you!* Tyler ran over to the group of boys gathered around the home plate of the baseball field—with Rico trailing behind him.

Who's your little buddy? Coach asked Tyler as he looked down at Rico. *I told you guys that you can't bring younger brothers, sisters, or cousins to practice.*

No, Coach, said Tyler. *This is Rico. He moved in across the street from me and he's ten like the rest of us. He'll be starting fifth grade and wants to try out for our team. He can catch anything!*

A few of the boys smirked at each other. Coach held out his hand toward Rico and Rico shook it while he looked at the ground.

Sorry about that. Nice to meet you, Rico, said Coach. *Let's see you catch and throw a few. Why don't you take first base?* Rico looked at the other boys shyly and then took his position.

Hey, Coach! yelled a kid named Jason. *I thought I was playing first base this year!*

You'll have to earn it, Jason, said Coach. *I want to see what the new kid can do.*

Derek, a large boy with red hair and freckles, smirked and said, *Little Rico doesn't even look big enough to hold a glove, let alone catch a ball. Maybe he should try out for the Pee Wee team.*

The other boys laughed. Tyler also started to laugh, but stopped when he saw the sad look on Rico's face.

Cut it out, guys! Let's see some good sportsmanship, said Coach, beginning to throw balls to Rico. Rico caught every one, including fly balls and grounders. Coach was also impressed by how fast Rico could run around the bases. Next, it was Jason's turn. Coach threw the same number of balls, but Jason missed two pop flies and a grounder. While the boys stretched, Coach announced the starting players for tomorrow's practice game. Tyler would be playing second base and Rico would be playing first! Jason was not happy to learn that he going to be playing right field.

Coach gathered his clipboard, duffle bag, and water bottle and blew his whistle. *That's all for today, men. See you here at ten a.m. tomorrow. Make sure your parents sign the forms I gave you, and bring them with you to practice. No form, no play!* With that, Coach jogged off toward his car and the boys started to pack up their gear. As Tyler gave Rico a high five, Jason walked over to them and glared down at Rico.

Who do you think you are, you little twerp? said Jason while poking his finger into Rico's chest. *I was supposed to play first base this year! You'd better tell Coach you want to play a different position. I'm not gonna lose my place to some scrawny kid with girly hair!* Jason gave Rico a shove and Derek flipped Rico's baseball cap off and stomped on it. Rico's shoulders hunched and his eyes were wide with fear. If possible, he looked even smaller than before.

In a tiny voice, he looked up at Jason and said, *Sorry. I didn't mean to take your spot.* A few of the boys gave high fives to Jason and others slapped him on the back in support as they turned to leave.

STOP & THINK

Parents: Take a moment and ask your child what it is about Rico that makes him likely to be bullied by Jason?

See how many things your child can come up with, and then review what was discussed in the previous section. Kids are vulnerable to being bullied when they're new to a group or don't have many friends, when they can be made to feel bad about themselves (lack of self-confidence), and when they are different in some way (for example: size, appearance, intellectual or sports ability). Rico is new to the neighborhood, he exhibits body language that shows his lack of confidence, he is small for his age, and he has longer hair than the other boys. Rico also performed better than Jason at tryouts. Kids can be picked on when their abilities are better or worse than other kids in their group.

Ask your child what changes Rico could make so he is less likely to be a target for a bully.

Review with your child the importance of making friends, meeting new people, being proud of her abilities and appearance, and projecting positive body language. Teach your child not to let others make her feel bad about herself. Everyone has unique gifts.

Rico kicked the dirt with his foot. Tyler thought Rico might cry. Tyler grabbed their gear, bumped Rico's shoulder, and said, *Don't worry about it, man. Jason's just mad because you played better than he did. Coach won't move you.* Tyler wondered why the guys—his teammates for years—were giving Rico such a hard time. He was surprised at how mean they'd been. It happened so fast that Tyler didn't know what to do.

Rico looked at Tyler and said, *I don't even care about first base. I don't want to be picked on again. I'm not playing baseball.* The boys walked home in silence.

When they reached their houses, Tyler said, *Maybe tomorrow's practice will be better, Rico. You're too good to quit.*

Rico smiled slightly and said, *Thanks, man. I really wanted to play, but it's not worth it.* Rico walked across the street and went into his house.

STOP & THINK

Parents: Ask your child to describe how Rico must feel after what happened. How does Tyler feel? What could Tyler have said to the other boys to stick up for Rico? Why are some kids afraid to stand up to someone who is acting like a bully?

Teaching your child to imagine how others feel in certain situations is a wonderful way to develop his sense of empathy. Talk about a few strategies your child can use if someone says or does something mean to him, or to one of his friends. Help your child find language that's comfortable for him. Ask him what he might say if he saw kids picking on a new student at school. Some kids are afraid to stand up to kids who are acting like bullies because they don't want to become the next target. Others just don't want to get involved. Still others want to help, but they don't know what to do. Remind your child that his safety is the most important thing and that he should not confront a bully unless there are other friends or adults around to help him. He can also support the target by leading him away from the bully, inviting him to join his group of friends, or getting help from a teacher.

Tyler found his mom in the kitchen and told her about what happened at practice. She brought him a snack and juice and sat at the table with him.

She looked at Tyler and said, *I'm sorry to hear that those boys were so mean to Rico. I can see you're really upset.*

I know! I wanted to tell Jason and Derek to stop picking on him, but I didn't know what to say. And it seemed like all the guys were going along with them, Tyler said. *Now Rico wants to quit the team.* He put his head down on the table and sighed.

Tyler's mom ruffled his hair and said, *Honey, you know that I always have your back. Is there anything I can do to help? Do you want me to call Coach?*

I don't know. Coach always tells us about sportsmanship and how we have to stick together to be a good team. The guys sure didn't act like a good team today. I think Jason is really jealous of how good Rico can play. I feel so bad for Rico. He's one of my best friends!

Tyler's mom gave him a hug and said, *Maybe you should tell Rico how you feel, and let him know you have his back.*

Tyler walked over to Rico's house and knocked on the door. Rico came outside and Tyler said, *Rico, I was thinking about what happened today. The guys on the team were really mean, and you didn't deserve to be treated that way! You're one of my best friends and I want to help make this right. You can't quit the team. We've been practicing all summer! Please come to the game with me tomorrow.*

Rico smiled shyly. Tyler could tell it felt good to Rico to know that Tyler had his back. *OK, I'll go to the game with you. But what if the guys—*

Tyler didn't even let Rico finish his sentence. *Don't worry about that. I've been thinking, and you should not let Jason, Derek, or anyone else make you feel bad about yourself. So what if you're smaller than the other guys? I've seen professional baseball and basketball players on TV who are smaller than the rest of their team members, and they're awesome players! Lots of guys have long hair like yours, too. None of that matters if you believe in yourself. And I'll be right there with you.*

The next day, Tyler and Rico walked to the park at 9:30 a.m. They were throwing a ball around when the other boys arrived.

Jason walked over to Rico and said, *What are you doing here, Pee Wee?* Derek snickered and grabbed Rico's glove, throwing it to Jason.

Rico took a deep breath. He looked Jason in the eyes and said, *Jason, give me back my glove!* Jason, surprised that Rico stood up to him, threw the glove to Derek.

Tyler stood behind Rico and said, *Jason, why are you being a jerk? Rico's new to our neighborhood, our school, and our team. How would you feel if you were a new kid and someone treated you like this?*

Jason's face turned red and he replied, *If I was a new kid, I wouldn't try out for a team like ours if I was a skinny runt like Rico.* Derek gave Jason a high five, but this time the other boys did not laugh. In fact, three of them walked over and stood with Tyler and Rico.

A boy named Elijah said, *Tyler's right, Jason. Being mean isn't cool. We're lucky to have Rico on our team. He's got skills!* Now the rest of the team stood with Tyler and Rico. Derek was the only one standing with Jason.

Tyler said, *Coach always tells us to show good sportsmanship and treat everyone with respect. We're never going to be a good team unless we learn that, and we're never going to win games if we don't support each other. Who's with me?* Tyler put his hand out, palm facing down. Rico put his hand on top of Tyler's. Elijah put his hand on top of Rico's, and all the other boys did the same until only Derek and Jason were left. Slowly, Derek reached out and put his hand on the top of the stack. Jason looked at all of the boys in the circle. It was obvious he realized the group had spoken by their actions, and even though Tyler could tell he didn't want to, he put his hand on top of Derek's.

The boys didn't notice that Coach had arrived and seen everything. He walked over and put his large hand on top of Jason's, saying, *I'm really proud of you, men. Tyler's right. You need to respect and support each other on and off the field. We all have strengths and weaknesses. While we practice to be good players, we should also practice to be good people. Now, let's line up at the fence for stretching before we run some laps.* All the boys groaned.

Tyler bumped shoulders with Rico, who flashed a huge grin. *Thanks,* said Rico.

I'll race you to the fence, said Tyler, and both boys took off running.

STOP & THINK

Parents: Ask your child what Rico did differently this time when Jason acted like a bully? How was Rico's body language different? Tyler was a bystander who became an upstander. Ask your child what those terms mean.

Discuss the importance of self-confidence. Remind your child that kids are often more effective than adults at stopping a bullying situation, and sometimes it only takes one child to stand up for someone who is being picked on before others will join in and help.

5

Skill-Building Activities for Adults & Kids

For Adults & Kids

Activities for Learning

These fun activities are really strategic exercises to help your child build skills and develop confidence, flexibility, and resilience, which are especially useful when kids are away from parents and home. The abilities to make friends, feel comfortable visiting other children's homes, try new activities, develop curiosity about kids from other cultures, and be aware of and sensitive to the emotions of self and others are foundational skills for independent development. Getting a good start on building positive relationships and recognizing behavioral boundaries goes a long way toward protecting your child from bullying.

Practice is essential for your child to become comfortable with the words and actions. It will definitely feel awkward the first few times. Keep working on it so your child will develop the skills to handle sticky situations. It's like training a muscle. If you never train it, it won't be strong when you need it. Have your child act out each strategy with you. At home, practice in front of a mirror, or use video to capture the fun. At school, students can work in small groups, taking turns with video recording, then sharing with the entire class.

These are seeds being planted for future action. We remember offering ideas to one of our daughters during the preteen years: *Why don't you say this? Do you think you could do that?* The reply: *Ohhhhh, Mommmmm* (insert eye roll here), *I could NEVER do (or say) that.* Three weeks later she was on the phone saying exactly what we'd discussed. Your child will find her own words if any of the ideas or words we offer don't sound like the way she would talk.

Pay attention to body language. Words offered with a smile and open body language can mean the exact opposite when said with arms crossed and rolling eyes. Here's where video is really effective. We often have no idea how we come across when we speak to others. Our words may say one thing and our body may be speaking a completely different language! Since body language accounts for 55% of the received message and words only account for 7%, it's important to make our body language match our words. Tone of voice accounts for 38%, so be careful about that, too. These are also very useful ideas for adults, when parenting and teaching.[16]

Children need to be aware of their surroundings to lessen their chance of becoming target. Talk with your child about safety in school, on the bus, and on walking routes. Avoid unsupervised areas. Always walk or play with at least one friend. Sit or remain in view of an adult (on the bus, in the auditorium, on the playground, etc.). If your child is being targeted repeatedly at school, a parent should speak to the adults in charge (teacher, bus driver) and give them a friendly (we mean friendly!) heads-up: *My son Erik is having a problem on the bus. Some of the older boys are calling him names. Can you keep an eye on what's going on? Thanks! I'll check back with you next week to see how it's going.*

Ideally, the *misbehaving* child should sit near an adult for extra supervision. To keep kids safe today, however, we must use practical strategies while we work to change behavior.

Activity 1

Getting to Know You & Building Trust

Parents: List three things you love about your child. What makes her unique? What are her talents? Why are you proud of her?

Kids: List three things you love about your parent (verbally, in writing, or by drawing pictures).

Share the lists with each other!

Teachers & Classes: Group students into pairs. Ask the kids to list three nice things about their partners. Share with the whole class.

Parents & Kids: Discuss what it means when you say you've "got your child's back." Reassure her that she can come to you with any problem, and you will work to solve it together.

Two pads of paper and pencils or markers are needed for this activity. Parent and child sit on the floor back to back. Without looking at each other, the parent draws a full-body picture of the child and the child draws a full-body picture of the parent. Show each other the pictures. The parent can cut out both images and the child can help to connect the hands of the parent and child drawings with tape to show their connection.

Teachers & Classes: Pairs of students sit back to back and draw full-body pictures of each other. With tape, connect the pictures of all the students in the class.

Activity 2

International Food Night at Home & Food Fair at School

This fun activity encourages diversity and acceptance, disguised as an enjoyable family cooking night. Pick a country whose food you would like to explore based on the cultural background of one of the kids in your child's class. Use the Internet—at home or in the library—to search for some easy recipes for a typical dinner. Plan it for a weekend, if that's an easier time. Your kids can share the responsibility by helping you find recipes, shop for ingredients, and do the kitchen prep work.

This is a learning activity on many levels. It gives kids a taste of international cuisine and unfamiliar foods, and it helps them experience what they might encounter when they visit a new friend whose family comes from another country. It's a wonderful chance to learn about new ingredients, pick up new kitchen skills when cooking together as a family, and discover some fun facts about nutrition and meal planning along the way. Travel your way around the culinary world!

This is also a great way to prepare your child to be a comfortable guest in someone else's home, where routines and foods will be different. Whatever the culture, if it's taco or sushi night, your kid will get a lesson in table manners and how to handle foods that can be messy or hard to eat in one bite. Teach your child, through practice, how to be more comfortable with awkward situations and ask for help: *Can you show me how to eat a crab?* Apologize and help clean up if he makes a mess: *Oops! Guess I need to try that again!* Practicing at home will make your child more confident and resilient when he ventures outside his normal comfort zones. The benefits of having an *"I can handle it"* mindset extend far beyond learning to use chopsticks!

Show your child, by example, how to have curiosity about and a sense of adventure for trying new foods (and meeting new people!), and how to handle, politely, the occasional *Now that I've tried it, it's not my favorite food* situation.

Extend this activity to the classroom or school. Many schools celebrate and build community with an international food fair, where every child brings a dish made at home that is based on the child's history or culture. This activity can be done with a single class or the whole school. Request copies of all recipes and be aware and considerate of allergies.

Activity 3

Meeting New People: Using Positive & Strong Body Language

Kids are often shy when meeting new people— other kids or, especially, adults. Teaching kids how to greet others helps encourage strong body language in other areas, too.

Why do we want strong and positive body language? There are at least two reasons: (1) You make a positive impression by looking like you're really interested to meet the new person, and (2) Kids with weak body language look like easy targets for bullying.

Teach your child the four parts to a strong greeting:

1. **Make Eye Contact**. Look right in the person's eyes as you approach.

2. **Offer a Handshake**. Kids will need to learn to shake hands with adults, although they'll usually skip this when meeting peers, or replace handshakes with high fives or fist bumps. Take the opportunity to practice so it's comfortable to use when they're meeting adults. Use a firm handshake with your whole hand. No wet-noodle or limp-finger handshakes here!

3. **Say Some Welcoming Words**. Say you're glad to meet them, or (for older kids) that you already have something in common: *Nice to meet you. I know Sarah, too. Your dad works with my dad. I saw you at dance class last week.* Speak with a firm, clear voice, loud enough to be heard.

4. **Smile.** This is the most important part. A smile says you're friendly and approachable.

This is another "planting the seeds" opportunity that may seem difficult at first. Mastering ice-breaking skills makes it easier for children to take the next steps to friendship and gives them some tools for speaking more easily with adults. When kids meet kids, they'll be less formal: a big smile, eye contact, and a *'Sup?* are just as friendly and welcoming as a more formal greeting.

This activity is a great chance to use video as a learning tool. If you have video available, record yourself and your child using weak body language (slumped shoulders, no eye contact, small voice). Then try a greeting with strong body language (smile, eye contact, strong handshake). Ask your child to describe the differences he can see.

Activity 4
Building the Vocabulary of Emotion

Children often know only three emotions: happy, sad, and mad. They need to know more, to be able to describe a fuller range of human feelings, and to be able to recognize them in themselves and others.

Make a list of 10 emotions. You can search online for a one-page handout of emotions with drawings of facial expressions. Some websites have pictures of facial expressions showing the range of universal emotions. You can also find online games to help children learn to recognize emotions.

This can be an especially challenging exercise for children with Autism Spectrum Disorder and other neurological problems. With repetition and support from adults, the gains these children make will be worth the extra effort.

Grab your video camera or phone, or stand in front of a mirror, and act out the emotions with your child. When you're acting out an emotion, be sure to use both your face and body language. You'll see something interesting—the same emotion might look different on your face than it does on your child's. For example, what might look like sadness on a child's face might actually be the feeling of fear.

Experiment with the size of the emotion. Be a little sad, medium sad, or catastrophically crushed. Try positive emotions, too—faintly amused, moderately entertained, or side-splittingly engulfed in laughter. What do your eyes do? How does your voice sound? What about your breathing? Our emotions influence our body systems.

Learning to read facial expressions is a really helpful skill in being able to recognize if another child has been hurt by playful teasing that's gone a bit too far. Teach her to ask: *Are you OK? What are you feeling? Are you feeling sad?* Remind your child that even if she's "only kidding," her words or actions could be hurting another person's feelings, and that's not OK.

This activity scales up easily for classroom use. Divide the class into groups of four. Video and replay, or act out the emotions within and between groups.

Activity 5

Being New or Meeting New Kids at School

New kids are more likely to be bullied. They don't have many friends yet and their lack of familiarity with the new environment and social structure makes them vulnerable. You don't want your kid to be a bullied new kid. And you don't want your kid to bully new kids. Let's stop both of these bad outcomes before they start.

Use the skills for meeting new people from Activity 3. For both new kids and "old," reaching out to meet someone new helps a new kid fit in and teaches your "old" child to do the right thing, even when it feels a bit awkward. Remind your child to show a new kid around the school, introduce him to other kids, and invite him to sit together at lunch. Include new kids in after-school activities—birthday parties, playdates, clubs, etc.

Bullying decreases inside the school when kids get to know one another better outside of school. While school is a great place for friendships to start, relationships deepen outside of school, both in pairs and in small groups.

Parents can significantly support this process by inviting each student in your child's class home to play, one at a time, over the course of the year. This plan works well for new kids, kids with friendship issues, and, actually, for all kids. It really reduces bullying when your child interacts one-on-one with every child in his class, even for 10 minutes.

It's surprisingly manageable. You're probably already doing it, but you just need to widen your child's circle. It's one of the best methods for helping your child build friendships and decrease bullying. While making school lunches, talk with your child about whom to invite this week. When you're walking or driving kids home from after-school activities, invite one or two children home each week, either after school or on weekends. Start by inviting any kids new to the class.

When kids visit your home, have some games, sports equipment, and (most important) yummy, healthy snacks planned. Choose activities that encourage kids to talk and cooperate. They will learn about one another and identify common likes and experiences. Video games may be a great way to break the ice when kids arrive, but set a time limit of 20–30 minutes. Video games and other forms of disconnected, parallel play put limitations on building in-depth friendships. If you leave your home with the kids, go where the kids can keep talking (a car ride, the park, food shopping, or out for a snack).

It's great when your child goes to another child's house, but you'll learn more when the playdates are on your turf—where you can easily see the ease or difficulty of friendship between the two children. Extend the friendship to the other child's family, especially if they are newcomers. Invite the rest of the family for a potluck dinner on a weekend.

Activity 6

New Kids at School: Special Tips for Teachers

While we're on the topic, let's focus in on the important role teachers and schools play in helping new students fit in, make friends, and be protected from bullying. Most schools have some procedures for new students—invite the new student to stand up and introduce herself to the class, and assign classmate buddies to make sure the new child finds her way to class, lunch, and recess.

Buddies, ambassadors, and pals are all excellent, but our efforts to support new children need to last far beyond the first week of school. It can take 3–6 months for a child to feel completely settled in her new school. Assign rotating ambassadors for 3–5 days until the new child has had a chance to buddy up with everyone in the class and be introduced to numerous circles of friends. Teachers can gently monitor the new friendships. Some schools have created inventive games for the new child to hunt for "treasures" (a new pencil) by finding and speaking to certain teachers, the librarian, the school secretary, and other adults around the school. Adding fun and playfulness can ease the transition and help a child build secure friendships in her new environment. The time spent doing this pays big dividends in classroom behavior. We're developing a cohesive class and teaching our values of making a place for and helping one another.

Activity 7

Recognizing & Choosing Positive Friendships

Read children's books with themes about friendship, empathy, respect, and bullying prevention. Don't be afraid to pick short books with simple stories, even for older children. Choose from this list of our favorite children's books, or find your own books about these important topics:

- *The Best Friends Book* by Todd Parr (Little Brown Books for Young Readers, 2000).

- *Billy the Baaadly Behaving Bully Goat* by Staci Schwartz (ComteQ Publishing, 2012).

- *Chester's Way* by Kevin Henkes (Greenwillow Books, 1988).

- *Feelings* by Aliki (Greenwillow Books, 1986).

- *Frog and Toad Are Friends* by Arnold Lobel (HarperCollins, 2003).

- *How to Be a Friend: A Guide to Making Friends and Keeping Them* by Laurie Krasny Brown and Marc Brown (Little Brown Books for Young Readers, 2001).

- *The Hundred Dresses* by Eleanor Estes (HMH Books for Young Readers, 2004).

- *The Invisible Boy* by Trudy Ludwig (Knopf Books for Young Readers, 2013).

- *The New Bear on the Block* by Staci Schwartz (ComteQ Publishing, 2006).

- *The Sneetches* by Dr. Seuss (Random House, 1961).

- *Stand in My Shoes: Kids Learning About Empathy* by Bob Sornson (Love and Logic Press, 2013).

- *Toot & Puddle: You Are My Sunshine* by Holly Hobbie (Little Brown Books for Young Readers, 2010).

- *Yo! Yes?* by Chris Raschka (Scholastic, 2007).

Parents: Read any of these books with your child.

Teachers & Classes: Create groups of 3–4 students and assign one book to each group. Make sure there's at least one capable reader in the group. This activity provides a perfect opportunity to bring older children to your classroom as "book buddies," to read to the younger students.

Parents & Teachers: Discuss and evaluate the story's friendships and relationships. Here are some ideas:

- Discuss each character in the story. Which characters are good friends? Why? Are any of the characters not acting like good friends? Why?

- Ask your child or students to make a list of five things that make someone a good friend. How do good friends make you feel? What would you do if a friend hurt your feelings? What do the faces of friends look like when they are play or talking? How do they talk to one another? Do good friends have to like all the same things? Do they ever fight? If they do, how do they solve the problem?

- If one of the books has a character who acts like a bully, ask your child or students to identify the bad or mean behavior. How do the other characters handle the situation? Do they stick up for the target and act like upstanders, or do they say nothing or encourage the bully by being bystanders?

- Discuss the bullying behavior of the characters. Take turns guessing why that character might be behaving that way. Remind your child or students not to be mean to, or exclude, bullies. Everyone deserves to be treated with kindness and respect, even while they are working to change their behavior. Don't bully the bully—it's easier for someone to change when they feel accepted.

- Ask your child or students what they would do if someone acting like a bully picked on them. What would they do if they saw one of their friends being picked on?

In the future, as you read other books with your child or class, take some time to focus on the feelings of the characters. How does the action of the story make the characters feel? How does it make the reader feel? Learn to identify the characters' facial expressions and emotions from illustrations to enhance emotional knowledge and empathy.

Activity 8

Be a Good Friend to Yourself: Positive Self-Talk

Teach your child about positive self-talk. Do you remember *The Little Engine That Could?* The tiny train was able to carry his heavy load up the mountain because he kept saying over and over, *"I think I can. I think I can. I think I can."* That's positive self-talk.

Many thoughts go through our minds. Help your child learn to recognize whether those thoughts are positive, neutral, or negative. If you both keep a journal for a few days, you'll be surprised to see what floats through your brains! Over time, your brain can be re-trained to think positive thoughts by becoming aware of negative thoughts as they occur and replacing them with positive statements. It's a great exercise for the whole family.

Here are some examples of positive self-talk:

- I'm a good person, and I deserve to be treated with kindness and respect.

- I'm a good friend.

- I'm kind to other people.

- I'm very funny.

- I like myself.

- I love challenges!

- I'm really good at _____.

- This seems hard, but I'll figure out a way to make it work!

- I know I'll find the answer to this math problem if I try again.

Practice saying some of these positive self-talk statements aloud with your child. Create some of your own positive self-talk statements and share them with each other.

Activity 9

Handling Conflicts & Disagreements

Conflicts are an inevitable part of life. In fact, some conflict is actually good. It adds complexity, diversity, and interest to our lives. Life would be pretty boring if we had no differences, everyone was the same, and we had no conflicts. The key is to limit conflicts and resolve them early before they go too far and damage relationships.

Start teaching conflict resolution skills when kids are young. Sibling sparring is usually a child's first opportunity to develop conflict-handling skills! For young children, use a simplified picture list of problem-solving choices. Post it on your refrigerator, or in your classroom.

Here are typical problem-solving choices for a kindergarten crowd, ages 4–5:[17]

- Talk

- Listen

- Share

- Take turns

- Get help

- Say *I'm sorry*

- Do nothing, or ignore the conflict

Make your own chart with your child, finding pictures to illustrate the conflict-solving choices. When a conflict arises between children, walk them to the chart and start the discussion by asking, *Which of the choices would you like to use to solve this conflict?* For pre-reading children, review the choices—the words that go with the pictures—and then help the children come to a solution.

With a lot of practice, children will remember the choices and no longer need to walk over to the chart. They'll be able to solve simple problems on their own with little adult intervention. That's the goal!

Activity 10

Dealing Directly with Bullying Behaviors

Even with all the practice in building friendship skills, life's not perfect. There will likely be times when bullying still occurs. Your child needs to know a variety of skills to stop or escape from uncomfortable situations before they escalate. **Please remember: The responsibility for creating safe, bully-free environments** *always* **rests with the adults.** Mistakes will still be made and kids will continue to test the limits until they are sure that "No Bullying Here" is really the rule. In an environment of respect for self and others, mistakes get fixed quickly and the rules—and positive peer pressure—bring behavior back in line before damage is done.

Here are some useful tips for your child to confront, dismiss, and stop bullying behavior:

- **Ignore it.** It's normal to get upset if someone does or says something mean. Kids who act like bullies feel powerful when they make targets upset, so a good first response is to ignore the bully's bad behavior and walk away. This can work, especially if your child has some friends who will support and walk away with her. Sometimes, however, the kid acting like a bully will say or do something worse to get attention. In that case, your child may have to find an adult or try another strategy.

- **Stand up to the kid who's acting like a bully**. Always think about safety first. Make sure that you are not alone and that you can get help from friends or grown-ups if you decide to stand up to a bully. Here's how you do that:

  - Take a deep breath.

  - Stand up tall with your head up and shoulders back.

  - Look the kid who's acting like a bully in the eyes.

  - Say in a firm, calm voice (without yelling): *Stop saying (or doing) that. I don't like when you call me names. That's mean.*

  - Walk away and join other friends, or find a teacher.

- **Set limits and walk away**. You can say: *I don't like how you're treating me. I'll come back when you stop being mean.* You're setting limits more gently while giving the kid who's acting like a bully a chance to change.

- **Use humor**. Sometimes humor can be an effective way to stop bullying. Saying something funny can show you aren't affected by the mean words and can shift the attention away from the bullying kid. For example:

    Bullying kid: *You're such a chicken!*

    You: *I am? Are my feathers showing?*

    Make sure the joke doesn't make fun of the kid who's bullying. Humiliating the bully is wrong and can make kids who act like bullies more aggressive.

- **Neutralize, don't challenge**. If you're not comfortable standing up to the kid who's acting like a bully, you can say something that doesn't directly challenge that person but still gives you something to say back before you walk away.

    Bullying kid: *You're such a baby!*

    You: *That's your opinion. Gotta go.*

Practice these responses with your child so they find their own words that feel more comfortable.

Parents often ask: Should I directly contact the parents of the child who is bullying? It seems like a great idea—to handle the problem simply between the parents of the two children involved. Unfortunately, it's rarely successful. Many parents are caught off-guard and react defensively when confronted, however calmly, with the thought that their child might be bullying *(Not my Emma!)*. We recommend that you don't directly approach the other child's parents unless you know them well. Even then, if they do not respond by saying, *Wow, thanks so much for telling us. Let's fix this,* then back off and ask the teacher or coach to take the lead.

Help your child identify supportive friends and remind her to seek help from an adult when necessary. Through casual problem-solving, guide your child to identify the best adults at school and after-school activities to seek out if your child or someone around her needs help. Do this before a problem arises—you'll be teaching your child the skills of proactive assessment. Check in with your child frequently about friendships, project groups, circle time, and how things are going on the playground. Encourage her to brainstorm solutions with you before you jump in and tell her what to do in every situation. Help your child build strength and skills.

Finally, always reassure your child by saying: *I've got your back!*

6

Going Forward: Skills for Life

For Adults

Skills for Life

Pencils? Check! Erasers? Check! Ruler? Check! Self-confidence? Check! Bullying prevention skills? Check!

Like organizing your supplies and homework before school, preparing your child's "inner game" will have a huge impact on how he will meet the challenges of the day—and the year ahead. While it may seem cute or precocious to think of a six-year-old "bringing his A-game" to first grade, his emotional intelligence and social-skill level—even at this age—are proven indicators of success in later life.[18] Building a solid inner game actually takes a lifetime.

You're making great progress! You and your child have taken big strides along that road by mastering the concepts and activities from this book: building the early skills of emotional awareness; strengthening your family's values of kindness, respect, and empathy; and practicing verbal and physical techniques that build confidence and competence for children. While reading this book with our kids, we've had many great opportunities to refresh our own adult inner game.

Your child's accomplishments—and yours—are just the beginning. Going forward, be alert to the many "teachable moments" and the better and worse behavior choices that present themselves in everyday life. These daily challenges—and occasional moments of *What should I do now?*—bring life to learning and help us practice, cement, and expand skills learned through reading and rehearsing. Adults should always be prepared to protect, include, and welcome a child who needs help. Make every day Bullying Prevention Day.

Our strongest skill is perhaps our gentlest. Compassion for ourselves and for others is the cornerstone. We must first accept our own strengths and weaknesses, even as we strive to keep growing and learning. Being gentle with others in the face of their mistakes and weaknesses is required if we want others to show compassion and support for our mistakes. Mistakes are wonderful opportunities to learn and to do better the next time. Compassion contributes to resilience.

People worldwide are suffering from feelings of isolation, disconnection, depression, and loneliness. Our kids are surrounded by examples of bad behavior at every level of society. Bullying occurs on popular reality shows, in cartoons and children's books, even in the race for the highest office in the United States—a world leadership position. We can and should hold ourselves to higher standards.

Friendship, empathy, and acceptance go a long way toward connecting people through compassion—one soul at a time. Commit to being part of this wave of change by teaching children, at the earliest ages, to move toward kindness and away from bullying.

We have provided you and your children with the opportunity to build important skills for creating positive friendships and relationships. We hope you will continue to practice, put these ideas into action, and continue growing. Surround yourself with friends who celebrate who you are and enrich your lives. Move away from— and minimize the impact from—unkind frenemies whose "friendship" comes at too high a cost. Teach your children to be comfortable in their own skins and have the inner strength to walk away from unkind, diminishing relationships.

We've helped you identify a structure for shaping children into kindhearted, resilient adults. Boys and girls can become, and surround themselves with, emotionally generous friends who will support and accept one another—overlooking one another's minor faults, focusing on and supporting one another's strengths, and encouraging the pursuit of big dreams. That's also an important part of the job description of parents and teachers!

This book has also provided an opportunity for adults to look at our own friendships through a new lens. Are we kind, respectful friends? Do we accept family and friends for who they are, including their imperfections? Do we put limits on, or move away from, toxic or negative relationships? Do we accept ourselves flaws and all, even as we strive to improve and grow? Being kind to ourselves is a good place to start.

It's time for action. Let's clean up our adult world and be living examples for our kids. We're all in this together.

Inspire, enrich, and collaborate!

With respect,

Lorna & *Staci*

7

Resources

Books

Blumen, L. *Bullying Epidemic: Not Just Child's Play*. Toronto: Camberley Press, 2011.

Blumen, L. *Bullying Epidemic 2: How Parents & Teachers Can Stop Bullying In Schools*. Toronto: Camberley Press Ltd, 2013.

Blumen, L. *Girls' Respect Groups: An Innovative Program to Empower Young Women & Build Self-Esteem!* Toronto: Camberley Press Ltd, 2009.

Blumen, L. *Girls' Respect Groups 2: No More Mean Girls!* Toronto: Camberley Press Ltd, 2013.

Coloroso, B. *The Bully, the Bullied & the Not-So-Innocent Bystander*. Toronto: HarperCollins, 2015.

Coloroso, B. *Extraordinary Evil: A Brief History of Genocide*. Toronto: Viking Canada, 2007.

Coloroso, B. *Just Because it's Not Wrong Doesn't Make it Right*. Toronto: Viking Canada, 2005.

Schwartz, S. *Billy the Baaadly Behaving Bully Goat*. Margate, NJ: ComteQ Publishing, 2012.

Schwartz, S. *The New Bear on the Block*. Margate, NJ: ComteQ Publishing, 2006.

See Chapter 5, Activity 7 for additional children's books.

Websites

ActAgainstViolence.APA.org

AutismSpeaks.org

Bullying.org

BullyingEpidemic.com

EraseBullying.ca

GirlsRespectGroups.com

KidsAreWorthIt.com

PacerTeensAgainstBullying.org

ParentingScience.com

Prevnet.ca

SafeYouth.org

StaciSchwartz.com

State.NJ.US/Education/Holocaust

StompOutBullying.org

StopABully.ca

StopBullying.gov

Endnotes

[1] Limber S., Olweus, D., and Luxenberg, H. *Bullying in US Schools 2012 Status Report.* Hazelden Foundation, 2013.

[2] Ibid.

[3] Hamm, M., Newton, A., Chisholm, A., et al. "Prevalence and Effect of Cyberbullying on Children and Young People: A Scoping Review of Social Media Studies." *JAMA Pediatrics*, 2015; 169(8): 770-777.

[4] Blumen, L. *Bullying Epidemic: Not Just Child's Play.* Toronto: Camberley Press, 2011.

[5] Blumen, L., Evans, N., and Rucchetto, A. *Girls' Respect Groups: An Innovative Program to Empower Young Women & Build Self-Esteem!* Toronto: Camberley Press, 2009.

[6] This chapter draws on previously published work by the author. Blumen, L. *Bullying Epidemic: Not Just Child's Play.* Toronto: Camberley Press, 2011.

[7] Beane, A. *The New Bully Free Classroom: Proven Prevention and Intervention Strategies for Teachers K–8*, 3rd ed. Minneapolis: Free Spirit Publishers, 2011.

[8] Hill, A. and Helmore, E. "Mean Girls," The Guardian, March 3, 2002. TheGuardian.com/education/2002/mar/03/schools.uk

[9] Coloroso, B. *The Bully, the Bullied, and the Bystander: From Pre-School to High School—How Parents and Teachers Can Help Break the Cycle of Violence.* New York: HarperCollins, 2002.

[10] Coloroso, B. Ibid.

[11] This chapter draws on previously published work by the author. Blumen, L. *Bullying Epidemic: Not Just Child's Play.* Toronto: Camberley Press, 2011.

[12] Gordon, S. "Bullies Target Obese Kids," *US News & World Report*, HealthDay, May 3, 2010. Health.USNews.com/health-news/family-health/brain-and-behavior/articles/2010/05/03/bullies-target-obese-kids.

[13] Kosciw, J., Greytak, E., Bartkiewicz, M., Boesen, M., and Palmer, N. *The 2011 National School Climate Survey: The Experiences of Lesbian, Gay, Bisexual, and Transgender Youth in Our Nation's Schools.* New York: Gay, Lesbian & Straight Education Network, 2012.

[14] Crisswell, P. *A Smart Girl's Guide to Friendship Troubles.* Middleton, WI: American Girl Publishing, 2013.

[15] Autism Speaks. AutismSpeaks.org.

[16] Thompson, J. "Is Nonverbal Communication a Numbers Game?" Psychology Today, September 30, 2011. PsychologyToday.com/blog/beyond-words/201109/is-nonverbal-communication-numbers-game.

[17] Kreidler, W. *Teaching Conflict Resolution through Children's Literature*. New York: Scholastic Professional Books, 1994.

[18] Mayer, J. and Salovey, P. "What Is Emotional Intelligence?" Salovey and Sluyter (eds.), *Emotional Development and Emotional Intelligence: Educational Implications*, 3-34. New York: HarperCollins, 1997.

Empower Kids & Prevent Bullying!

Billy the Baaadly Behaving Bully Goat

Staci J Schwartz, MD

Billy the Baaadly Behaving Bully Goat is a story, written in rhyme, about a young goat named Billy who constantly picks on the other "kids" in his class. From stealing their lunch money to pulling their hair, Billy is making life miserable for his elementary school peers. When Mr. and Mrs. Goat realize that they have exhausted all of their own strategies to stop their son's unacceptable behavior, they finally seek help from The Wise Old Goat, a certified Goat Therapist. With a little bit of magic dust, some common sense, and family support—a brilliant plan is initiated to cure Billy of his bullying ways. A Teacher & Student Activity Guide is also available for educators.

What's different about *Billy the Baaadly Behaving Bully Goat*?

- This story offers a solution to the problem of bullying that does not involve "bullying the bully." Instead, Billy learns how his *own* behavior affects other goats; he learns that *he* has the power to stop his bullying behavior.

- This story provides children with the opportunity to identify bullying behavior and share their personal experiences with bullying—either as an intimidator, a victim, or a witness.

- Many stories about bullies focus only on the victims/targets. The bully in this story also needs help and attention in order to change his behavior. This help may come from parents, teachers, principals, counselors, and therapists—and surprisingly, from the other kids!

Empower Kids & Prevent Bullying!

The New Bear on the Block

Staci J Schwartz, MD

The New Bear on the Block is a story, written in lighthearted rhyming verse, about the adventures of a tiny grizzly bear who moves to a small town in the woods. After a series of silly mishaps that occur when his glasses are accidentally broken, his new neighbors want to banish him for his perceived rude behavior. A wise turtle (the town optician), who meets the bear and finds him to be a delightful new friend, must correct the false perceptions of his fellow neighbors. He educates them about avoiding impulsive judgment of others based on erroneous first impressions and incomplete facts and teaches them that there are always other perspectives from which they can view a situation. A Teacher & Student Activity Guide is also available for educators.

What's different about *The New Bear on the Block*?

- This story promotes discussions about how to be a good friend, welcome a new neighbor (classmate, team member, or colleague) into a community, avoid impulsive judgment of others, and embrace change with a positive attitude.

- The characters' actions will teach children about the disadvantages of jumping to conclusions and succumbing to a "gang mentality" when they are part of a group.

- The book's conclusion teaches young kids that there is always more than one side to a story and emphasizes the importance of apologizing for misconceptions and misunderstandings.

Empower Kids & Prevent Bullying!

Bullying Epidemic: Not Just Child's Play

Lorna Blumen

Bullying Epidemic: Not Just Child's Play **is a powerful book on children's bullying** and the enabling role adults inadvertently play. Belligerent adult behavior and silent acceptance of bullying all around us pave the way for children's bullying. Adults must change our behavior so children can change theirs.

Prevention is the only solution. We must start when the kids – and the problems – are small. Let it build and bullying becomes impossibly complex. While we must respond to the crises, the Columbines, and the bullycides, we cannot repair the damage with punishments, metal detectors, or jails.

We can prevent most of these crises. We must stop blaming legal loopholes and the inaction of others for our own failure to act. Tackling tough issues that others ignore, *Bullying Epidemic* offers a commonsense action plan for adults determined to turn the tide of children's bullying.

Empower Kids & Prevent Bullying!

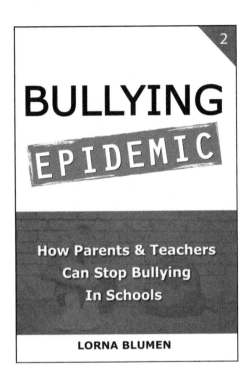

Bullying Epidemic 2: How Parents & Teachers Can Stop Bullying In Schools

Lorna Blumen

Why is bullying such a problem in schools and what can we do about it? *Bullying Epidemic 2: How Parents & Teachers Can Stop Bullying In Schools* provides action-oriented tips and practical strategies for adults determined to stop children's bullying. Developed for classroom use, these strategies are equally effective at home, camp, sports, or any place where kids work or play together.

You'll find tips and discussion starters from our 20 Tips for Bully-Free Schools Program, Bullying ABCs, How to Work With Your Child's School: A 10-Step Action Plan to Stop Bullying Problems, and 10 Tough Questions Parents Ask About Bullying.

Make Every Day Bullying Prevention Day!

Empower Kids & Prevent Bullying!

Girls' Respect Groups:

An Innovative Program to Empower Young Women & Build Self-Esteem!

Lorna Blumen, Natalie Evans, & Anne Rucchetto

Respect, for ourselves and others, drives our important life decisions – the friends we choose, how we approach school and work, the challenges we accept or avoid. Girls' self-respect is under attack from all sides today. How do we keep young women grounded in respect?

Welcome to the Girls' Respect Groups Program, now used in the US, Canada, and 130 countries. The GRG Program is an after-school program for preteen girls, run by specially-trained high school girls. Created by real teens, it's a community of Girls Helping Girls (our motto!). This book contains the complete GRG Middle School Program curriculum, guiding you step-by-step to build GRG Programs in your schools and communities. Identify and train inspiring teen girls to become confident, kind-hearted GRG Teen Leaders. The GRG Program is anchored by teachers and adult community leaders and a vibrant online community providing tips and encouragement. Help young women find their best selves and provide a stabilizing anchor during the turbulent teen years!

Empower Kids & Prevent Bullying!

Girls' Respect Groups 2: No More Mean Girls!

Lorna Blumen

Need a quick start guide for supportive girls' friendships? *Girls' Respect Groups 2: No More Mean Girls!* gives you key info from the Girls' Respect Groups Program, used in the US, Canada, and over 130 countries.

Adults must guide preteens and teens towards healthy friendships and romantic relationships. Action-oriented tips and practical strategies include Respect ABCs and Learn-A-Tip-A-Day infographics to inspire discussion and action. We cover challenging issues for all girls: What's the connection between respect and bullying? How do you make the best clothing choices? How to set the tone for respect during the dating years?

Girls 10 to 18 – and the adults who love and guide them – will learn to create relationships based on respect for self and others. *Girls' Respect Groups 2: No More Mean Girls!* is an important book for parents of boys, too. Help your sons choose girls, as friends or romantic partners, who respect themselves and your sons.

The Gift of Respectful Relationships Lasts a Lifetime!

Empower Kids & Prevent Bullying!

The Art of Followership:

How Great Followers Create Great Leaders and Organizations

Ronald Riggio, Ira Chaleff, Jean Lipman-Blumen, Editors

The Art of Followership examines the multiple roles followers play and their often complex relationship to leaders. With contributions from leading scholars and practitioners from the burgeoning field of leadership/followership studies, this groundbreaking book outlines how followers contribute to effective leadership and to organizations overall.

Drawing from various disciplines, from philosophy, psychology and management, and education, the book defines followership and its myriad meanings. *The Art of Followership* explores the practice and research that promote positive followership and reveals the part that followers play in setting the standards and formulating the culture and policies of the group.

The contributors include new models of followership and explore fresh perspectives on the contributions that followers make to groups, organizations, societies, and leaders. The book also explores the most current research on followership and includes insights and perspectives on the future of leader-follower relationships.

Lorna Blumen wrote Chapter 16: *Bystanders to Children's Bullying: The Importance of Leadership by "Innocent Bystanders"*. Publisher: Jossey-Bass. Book description from publisher's website.

When Something's Wrong: Ideas for Families

Canadian Psychiatric Research Foundation (now Healthy Minds Canada)

A quick reference guide of useful coping strategies and resources for parents and caregivers to help them with children who have mood, behavior, or thinking problems. This handbook (2004) includes twelve sections covering Managing Problem Behaviour in Children, Anxiety and Anxiety Disorders, Autism and Autism Spectrum Disorders, Borderline Personality Disorder (BPD), Eating Disorders, Impulse Control Disorders, Mood Disorders, Schizophrenia, Suicide, Tourette Syndrome (TS), Working with your Health Practitioner, and Resources.

Lorna Blumen was a contributing author to the Anxiety Disorders section. Publisher: Healthy Minds Canada. Book description from publisher's website.

CPSIA information can be obtained
at www.ICGtesting.com
Printed in the USA
LVOW05s0852280516

489994LV00021B/113/P